The Vatican

Behind the Scenes in the Holy City

Pope Pius XII celebrates Mass in St. Peter's Church

The Vatican

Behind the Scenes in the Holy City

by **Ann Carnahan**

with photographs

by **David Seymour**

FARRAR STRAUS and COMPANY · NEW YORK

𝔑𝔦𝔥𝔦𝔩 𝔬𝔟𝔰𝔱𝔞𝔱:

    JOHN M. A. FEARNS, S.T.D.
    Censor Librorum

𝔍𝔪𝔭𝔯𝔦𝔪𝔞𝔱𝔲𝔯:

    ✠ FRANCIS CARDINAL SPELLMAN
    Archbishop of New York

The nihil obstat and imprimatur are official declarations that a book or pamphlet is free of doctrinal or moral error. No implication is contained therein that those who have granted the nihil obstat and imprimatur agree with the contents, opinions or statements expressed.

Photographs edited and book designed by
NELSON GRUPPO

MANUFACTURED in the U.S.A.

The Murray Printing Company
Wakefield, Massachusetts

I AM ESPECIALLY INDEBTED to Mr. Franklin C. Gowen, Special Assistant to the Personal Representative of the President of the United States to His Holiness, Pope Pius XII, for his help and encouragement in preparing this book; to His Excellency, Monsignor Ludovico Kass of the Sacred Congregation of the Basilica of St. Peter and to His Excellency, Count Enrico P. Galeazzi, Director General of the Administrative and Economic Services of the Holy See—Special Delegate to the Pontifical Commission—Architect of the Sacred Apostolic Palaces.

A Message from Pope Pius XII

"THE CONFLICT between the good and the wicked, in whose ever-tangled strands of human actions and motives history is woven, has seldom, if ever, been so acute as it is today.

"While on the one hand, no matter where we look out upon the world from this Vatican citadel, we are filled with admiration and joy at the sight of the good people resplendent with those virtues, which, particularly in the glorious fortitude of martyrs, recall the early ages of Christianity: yet on the other, we are overcome by grief and anguish as we perceive the iniquity of the unrighteous reach a degree of impiety that is incredible and without parallel . . .

"Proud neglect and disdain of divine things . . . is the most pernicious source of all evils and at the present time is insidiously spreading its ravages almost all over the world like a virulent disease; it is producing evils without number, especially in those countries where a conspiracy has been formed 'against the Lord and His Christ' . . .

"It deprives man of God and thereby robs him of his spiritual dignity, makes him the ignoble tool of materialism and utterly destroys all traces of virtue, love, hope and beauty of soul within him. We speak of atheism or, rather, hatred of God . . .

"Let nothing give more concern to you . . . than battling to defend the name of God . . .

"Let us worship with the greatest earnestness and care God's loving presence in the sanctuary of a clear conscience . . .

"Let memory be filled with His most sweet presence; let the intellect be enlightened, the souls rejoiced and the will strengthened to act with purity, energy and piety . . . .

"And whoever is strong in faith and rich in the treasures of a religious life should share these goods, as far as possible, with others . . ."

Pius XII
Rome, 12 February, 1949—on the occasion of Joseph Cardinal Mindszenty's sentence to life imprisonment by a Hungarian court.

Contents

Introduction

AFTER MASS in the great cathedral down the street, His Eminence, Eugenio Cardinal Pacelli came to breakfast at the home of Archbishop John Glennon of St. Louis. It was the summer of 1936. Cardinal Pacelli, now Pope Pius XII, was the Secretary of State of the Holy See.

I knelt before him, one of a group. His smile, meant for all of us, was the gentle, faraway smile of an ascetic. But his deep eyes were not aloof, not cold; rather brilliant and magnetic. They carried the impact of a world force. His eyes rested on me for a moment.

This book began then. In the next twelve busy years, I dreamed of three things that I wanted to do at the Vatican.

I wanted to see again the man of the saintly but strong face who in 1939 became the Vicar of Christ.

I wanted to climb to the highest point in the great dome of St. Peter's Church, to see the whole of the world's smallest and in some ways most powerful state.

I wanted to walk about in the Holy City—see the sights—talk to some of the people who live and work in the place which has been world headquarters of the Catholic Church for twenty centuries.

And, being a writer, I wanted to write about it.

In July of 1948, I first went to Rome. I had a magazine assignment and ten days to cover it. I finished it in a week and had three days left over—three days to investigate two thousand years of the Vatican. Of course it didn't work, but I tried to follow the three points of my plan—and I did learn those things which made possible my work during the spring of 1949.

I first discovered that an audience with the Pope, on such short notice, was impossible. His Holiness was at Castelgondolfo on his one brief holiday of the year. This meant no vacation from his enormous responsibilities, but audiences were discouraged save for diplomats and church authorities.

After Mass on a Sunday morning, I tried for point two of my program.

The paths of pilgrims cross in St. Peter's Square in Rome

I walked to the entrance of St. Peter's basilica and, a bit to the left, waited for an elevator to take me to the cupola. The machine was in "seasonal disrepair," I was told finally by a passing San Pietrino (worker). Would I walk the more than a thousand steps straight up toward the broiling July sun? It was too much. I took my disappointment to the cool marble corridors of the Pinacoteca and tramped through three miles of the Vatican art collections.

The third point of my plan would be simple. I had read that the Holy City was so small one might walk across it, from wall to wall, in fifteen or twenty minutes. From a saints' calendar on my hotel room wall, I mapped for my last day in Rome an easy walking tour across the Vatican's 108 acres.

In the morning, a little after six o'clock, the matin bells were silent. From my window I could see most of Rome; in the distance lay the Tiber and beside it rose the dome of St. Peter's Church. Everything was quiet. Not just early-morning quiet but the uneasy hush of a general strike called the day before when Communist leader Togliatti had been shot while coming through the doorway of Italy's Chamber of Deputies. All Romans were keeping behind closed doors.

In the stillness, I set off across the empty streets on my way to see the miniature city-state that would fit on an 18-hole golf course.

The Piazza of St. Peter when I arrived was almost deserted. A few black-garbed priests and nuns in crisp starchy blue habits walked past me and climbed the steps to the church. There were none of the usual taxis or carriages. No postcard stands. No guides. The man who sold rosaries was not at his place.

The Swiss Guards were posted, as they have been for five centuries, at the Gate of the Bells. I told them in stumbling French why I was there before nine o'clock in the morning. They smiled and swung open the black-and-white-striped barrier of the Vatican frontier.

In the office for visitors' permissions, I explained again and showed my passport. On the first page my occupation was listed—"Journalist." "No," said the officer, "this 'Journalist' means you must make a request in writing to the authorities."

I protested, "But today I'm just a tourist."

The officer was sorry; but "no" was still the answer.

No audience with the Holy Father. No survey of the Vatican from the dome. No walking tour.

I went into the cool depth of the cathedral. I sat down quietly on a choir bench in the apse. A few pilgrims filtered through the dim light into the shafts of sunlight hovering around the great Bernini columns of the high altar. They peered down into the place of St. Peter's tomb. Boys in lace smocks came along to check the candles in a little chapel near the confessionals. The boys, as servants of the church, were free to come and go at will in the Holy City; the pilgrims and I were not. Still, I thought, millions of people would give much to be where we were, to see what we had already seen in the great Christian church founded near the spot of St. Peter's crucifixion.

After an hour on the choir bench, I walked slowly around. I saw with better eyes what I had seen the day before. As I stood near the heavenly mosaic copied from Raphael's "Transfiguration," a priest passed me and said, "Good morning."

We spoke of the treasures of the church and I asked about the construction shafts leading down into the crypts below.

"Are you English or American?"

"American," I said. And then suddenly I said much more—I told him all the story of my plans and how they had come to nothing.

"Father," I finished, "in this postwar turmoil, there are many new questions about religion in the minds of all of us. About the strength of the Roman Catholic Church—and the attacks on it. About the Holy Father. He is now something much more than the spiritual leader of the Roman Catholics; his plans and programs to promote peace affect all of us. Even the decisions he makes for his Church influence us. I am one of millions who want to know more about him. How he lives and works. Who works for him, with him. What is the daily life of the people in his little state? The Church may be twenty centuries old—but the Vatican City itself is just twenty years old; no one outside knows enough about it.

"In the Holy Year of 1949-50, they say 5,000,000 pilgrims will come to Rome. From England, France, Italy, South America, China, Japan, Africa and the United States. They will see St. Peter's and the art collections or the Library—just a part of the Vatican. Those who cannot travel to Rome will miss even that. Now I have seen a little, I want to know more. Others will be just like me. Why can't I—?"

The priest stopped me. "I think you can. Get help, from Vatican authorities, from your American Embassy people in Rome. If you really want to tell the story, it can be told."

Seven months later I flew back to Rome with photographer David Seymour and the hope that the friendly priest was right. For ten weeks we lived in the Vatican City—seven days a week from early morning, when the gates were unlocked to admit the first workmen and provisions, until late at night when they were barred against the city outside.

Mr. Seymour and I walked wall to wall, across country. Not once but many times to photograph and rephotograph the shops and stores and little back streets of the Holy City, to interview its citizens. We talked to workmen, cooks, and plasterers working three floors and seventeen centuries below the basilica. Repair artists doctoring the famous Raphael frescos, lawyers of the Sacra Rota, carpet cleaners in the Sistine Chapel and plainclothesmen of the Pontifical Guard became our friends. We called on officials in the Secretariat of State, cardinals, newsmen, the world's most famous bookworms and art authorities. We ate our lunch in the workers' canteen, cheered a soccer game at the Ethiopian College.

We were forbidden nothing. Day after day we were ushered through the maze of secret passages, locked gates, forgotten rooms, by an official guards' officer of the Vatican, assigned to us as an "angel," with instructions to help us find the best material for this book.

Six times I was in audience with the Holy Father. The first time I saw Eugenio Pacelli as Pius XII was on his birthday when he also celebrated the tenth anniversary of his election as Pope.

Yellow-and-white papal flags flew from almost every building in the Holy City on the morning of March 2, 1949, when I presented my formal invitation to the Swiss Guards at the Bronze Door. After a quick glance at my papers and a smart salute, I was permitted to climb shakily up the great stair to the Court of St. Damascus. At the elevator to the papal apartments, I was met by a footman. Through room after room, beautifully painted and decorated in red and gold and white, I followed my guide. Finally I was seated in the little red throne room, just five rooms away from the private office of His Holiness and had a chance to look around at the others who were to share my privilege. There were two Dutch nuns who in their nervousness said never a word; five fidgety Czech refugees, parents and three scrubbed and thin children, to whom the Holy Father later spoke for almost half an hour in German. And me.

Presently, we were joined by a young American couple with four children. The baby was carried in the mother's arms. As they were seated by a papal chamberlain, the infant wakened and began to howl. At a high note in his terrified wailing, the chamberlain came back to call the family into the next room for presentation to the Pope. The mother jumped up. She looked first at the chamberlain in his formal black broadcloth and lace, then at her sobbing young one. The chamberlain shook his head from left to right.

The mother glanced at the nuns, turned to me. "American?" she asked.

Five seconds later I was pacing the gold-and-rose-circled Aubusson carpet—ten times clockwise and ten reverse. I gently patted the back of my small charge; he cried still louder. I jiggled him up and down. Then I thumped him solidly and rhythmically until, after a half hour, he gave a large hiccup and sagged asleep. The Noble Guards in attendance grinned beneath their flaring mustaches.

The shoulder of my black dress was damp; the baby's tears had soaked the black silk rebozo I wore to cover my hair. My arms ached and I was warm with embarrassment when the mother hurried back into the room.

"Quick," she said as she retrieved her burden, "His Holiness says he doesn't care if the baby *does* cry!"

The last time I was received, on the day before I left Rome, I went with Mr. Seymour to the gold-and-white private study of the Holy Father. Neither one of us had ever been admitted there before. The purpose of our visit was a portrait of the Holy Father, which we were missing in our collection of 2500 pictures of life in the Vatican.

We were permitted to take the portrait. As we genuflected and prepared to leave the room, His Holiness said, "We understand the importance of your work. It has our blessing."

ANN CARNAHAN, *10 August, 1949, Rome*

15

In the Shadow of the Dome

An old italian proverb says a man born *"sotto il cupolone"* shall find his life's work there.

Eugenio Pacelli, Pope Pius XII, was born on March 2, 1876, "in the shadow of the dome" of St. Peter's. The day he was born his father Filippo carried the child in his arms to the great basilica where he was baptized in a font near the front entrance. According to old Roman law, use of this font as big as a bathtub is the special privilege and right of Roman children.

Although the Pacelli family came from a small town in Tuscany named Onano, they had been established in the city long enough to belong there, to think of their children, and bring them up, as Romans.

Eugenio as a little boy frequently went with Donna Virginia, his beautiful mother, to services in St. Peter's. The Pope had been locked up in the Vatican since 1870 when Victor Emmanuel captured Rome, but the first church of the Catholics was kept open and in use.

Accompanied by his brother Francesco, Eugenio sometimes walked around the ninth-century walls which were the boundaries of the Pope's self-imposed exile. The two boys hiked north from St. Peter's Square along the Via Angelica. They passed the Vatican back door, St. Anna Gate, and when they reached the Piazza del Risorgimento, turned left. In winter, they kept close under the turrets and towers of the wall, out of the biting wind. They

In the shadow of the dome, a street carnival in full swing

Outside the walls of the Holy City,
a balloon vendor waits
for his young Italian customers

walked at a fast pace along Viale del Vaticano as it climbed the slope of
Vatican Hill to get a better view of the Swiss sentries on the battlements.

In spring, they ambled. Street fairs and markets were set up along the
curb. New fruits and fresh flowers were hawked, and songbirds were on
sale. Trained mice swung from hemp ribbons or climbed little wooden steps
built into their cages. On every corner families and their friends gathered
to enjoy the Roman sunshine and listen to the street musicians sing. The
short hour's walk circling the zigzag walls became a half-day excursion.

Because he was the son of a good patrician family and it was customary, young Pacellino entered the "small clergy" and assisted the priest
almost daily. It is said that the boy often rushed from the church of the
Filippini near his home to "say" as much of the Mass as he could remember

18

to his little sister. Then he would seat her on a nursery chair and deliver fiery extemporaneous speeches on the trials of the poor walled-up popes— the problems their brother one day was to help solve.

Eugenio was enthusiastically pious, but his parents were not overly impressed. They sent him to an excellent non-Catholic school in Rome. In those days, this was considered a daring action for a family to take—one to be considered only when children were so firm in their faith that there could be no possible danger of any other doctrine being assimilated.

The rather frail young boy, who was already wearing spectacles, was a brilliant and original student; he took honors in history. While he climbed the regulation number of trees in the summertime, his city exercise consisted of the frequent walks in and about the neighborhood of St. Peter's.

Along the Via del Conciliazione which runs from St. Peter's Square

**Getting ready for the Holy Year and pilgrims:
The Via della Conciliazione leading to
St. Peter's is widened and repaved**

**Vatican real estate holdings—
a line of buildings across the street from
the Holy City and belonging to it**

**Under construction—a large, modern
hostel for priests and pilgrims
who will visit Rome during the Holy Year**

three city blocks to the Tiber, there is history on every corner. This street
did not exist in 1890—the area was a network of mean, badly planned streets
centuries old—but the landmarks were much as they are now.

There was the Convertendi Palace once owned by Raphael and re-
decorated by Bramante, the great Vatican architect. A few feet farther along
was the Torlonia Palace where Henry the Eighth of England housed his
ambassadors to the Holy See until he fell out with Rome over his multiple
marriages.

In an alley off the Borgo Pio—the borough built by Pius IV in 1561
—there was and is still an ancient bell foundry. Belonging to the family
Lucenti, it has been active since Bernini gave the order to cast the columns
for the high altar in St. Peter's—and had the bronze stolen from the

A branch of the Banco Santo Spirito (Bank of the Holy Ghost) plastered with Communist posters and voting notices

On the sunny side of the Via della Conciliazione, the San Pietro café with tables outside for tourists to lunch, drink St. Peter's beer

Pantheon to do it. Three hundred years ago the Lucenti foundry also made for Bernini the *Predica*, the sweet and solemn-toned bell that today rings out the Easter Mass.

Right on the Tiber, there is the Palace of the Banco Santo Spirito, one of the world's oldest banking institutions. Close by, where the modern bridge of Victor Emmanuel crosses the river, is the site of the first Vatican bridge. In a Roman kind of WPA project, Rome proper was connected with Vatican Hill to make it simpler for townspeople to consult the priests there who read omens or foretold the future from the flight of birds. When Vatican bridge was finished more than two thousand years ago, it was placed under the supervision of the pagan priests who assumed the name of *pontefici* or pontiffs, the bridge builders. The Holy Father's title of *Pontifex Maximus*, master bridge builder, was used by Roman emperors and the first bishops of Rome before it belonged to the popes as heads of the Church.

In this low, once swampy district along the river—as far north as the fortress Sant' Angelo—the Christians and Jews of the first century after Christ were herded. When Simon called Peter arrived in Rome about A.D. 42, he lived and taught in the midst of these poverty-stricken colonies.

Roman citizens and writers of that era were bitter in their denunciation of Jews. Because Christians lived with them side by side, Jewish persecution included the followers of Peter. It is thought that many of the great blocks of marble now built into St. Peter's basilica, but originally intended for pagan temples on Vatican Hill, were hewn by Jews and Christians, banished to the mines of Carrara in an early wave of oppression.

The burning of Rome in the year 64 fanned the hate against the Christians that had begun to smolder. Legend now blames the Emperor Nero for the blaze, but at the time the Christians were accused of being the incendiaries. As law then punished fire by fire, Christian martyrs were burned—frequently on Vatican Hill, in large groups, at night.

Hunting down members of the new religion became a popular sport. Nero, who disposed of his mother, wives and friends with unparalleled *sangfroid*, devised some of the more horrible methods by which the believers died to divert the Emperor's friends. Christians were tossed like crackers to wild animals in the arena. They were tarred and feathered and set afire while mad, drunken Nero drove his chariot around and around the circus he had built on Vatican Hill. Following the disciple of Christ of Nazareth was hazardous and conversion was only for the brave.

By the year 67 when Peter himself fell into the hands of the persecutors, the faith was as steadily anchored as the rock on which Christ had founded his church. His followers were hardy. They lived in the mountains, in the wet cellars along the river. They hid in the catacombs outside the city walls. They fought. They prayed. They taught others.

His work in the main accomplished, the first Bishop of Rome died on the sand of Nero's circus, the site of St. Peter's Square. Surrounded by unholy shrines and a pagan playground, Peter chose to be crucified head down. He believed himself unworthy to die in the same manner as his Divine Master.

The sixteenth-century Pauline walls of the Holy City under repair

22

St. Peter's Church

THE VERY OLD PROFESSOR NEVIANI was still alive when his former pupil Eugenio Pacelli was elected 262nd successor to St. Peter and Supreme Pontiff of the Church. He liked to remember the studious youth.

"I could draw a blueprint of the Collegio Romano. And I can still see the pupil Pacelli. He sat in the second row, second form. We knew him to be of promise. And my heart told me that something quite wonderful was going to happen.

"I can remember that his teacher of Italian, the exceptional Ildebrando

Nuns and a priest gaze at the imposing façade of the Church of St. Peter

della Giovanna, liked Pacelli very much and esteemed him for his lively intelligence, his firm will and application to his work. The judgment of such a teacher was all I needed."

The promising student applied himself with such zeal to his studies at the Capranica College for priests that he was forced to drop out. Away from his beloved Rome, he read and rested until the family doctor promised the immediate danger of tuberculosis was past.

Then with others of his age, including his best friend Luigi Maglione, he learned philosophy, theology, canon and civil law. On his way up through the Gregorian University and the exclusive Pontifical Seminary, he spent less time in the neighborhood of the Vatican—and more time in it.

The Holy City became his second home. Few days passed when the tall, aristocratic young student did not swing across St. Peter's Square—the front porch of that world.

For sale: sheets bearing the portraits of former popes in miniature. Behind the Italian hawker, statues of saints lined against the sky

A thriving business in postcards, maps of the Holy City, guide and picture books is done daily at the counters and stands in St. Peter's Square

Photograph originally taken for Look Magazine

**Special for Palm Sunday—palms to be blessed
are offered those entering church; palms
already blessed to those coming out from Mass**

**Siesta in the noonday sun. An Italian laborer
sleeps against one of the great Bernini
columns which encircle St. Peter's Square**

As an Italian he enjoyed the hurly-burly of the Square and the hour-to-hour busyness of all the people who met there. As a Roman, he delighted in the traffic to the great church. His trained history sense made acute his appreciation of the life for which he was headed. He loved his work; he loved people. The two seemed one at St. Peter's.

Today, as Pope Pius XII, he looks from his second-story study windows down on the Square. The horse-drawn hacks of fifty years ago have been replaced by shiny green taxis, but the stands selling mementos and rosaries are as they were. The great fountains still spray the pavement for fifty yards on a windy day. Young lovers stroll in the curved *allée* between the Bernini columns and are careful not to disturb the babies who sleep in their prams or the old men eating their bread and Bel Paese cheese.

The pilgrims and the tourists with their cameras cluster about the base of the obelisk the better to "shoot" the façade of the church. This shaft of white marble mounted in the center of the square of St. Peter was brought from Egypt long ago by Caligula. It later stood in Nero's circus. It lasted centuries after the circus had been torn down and other buildings constructed on the hill.

In the sixteenth century, Sixtus decided to move the monument to its present location, to the spot where the disciple is supposed to have been crucified. As the piece weighs more than 300 tons, Sixtus asked advice from

Students, priests, American sailors and tourists—pilgrims from every land are ardent camera fans in the Square of St. Peter

Curious visitors peek through the open Bronze Door past a Swiss Guard

hundreds of architects and engineers on the method of transfer. Domenico Fontana's suggestion of lowering the shaft to a horizontal position, sliding it over wooden rollers and then hoisting it upright was adopted.

On September 10, 1586, the Pope and his court with thousands of onlookers took their positions in front of the basilica. On threat of punishment by death, the crowd was silent as many great windlasses and eight hundred men started to pull at the obelisk.

Suddenly—the winches winding on, the stone shaft stopped in mid-air and the ropes began to burn. An Italian sailor among the workers called, "Wet the ropes." Just as the papal police closed in on the offender, buckets of water were dashed over the smoking lines and the obelisk settled gently to the spot where it stands today. The sailor, whose name was Bresca, was pardoned by the Pope, and his family, since they came from a town famous for its palm trees, were granted, for all time, the privilege of supplying palms for St. Peter's on Palm Sunday.

Eugenio Pacelli never saw the famous Bronze Door, through which pilgrims pass to audience with him, open until February of 1929. At this time the Vatican's territorial rights were re-established by treaty and concordat with Mussolini.

But there were other entrances opening to him. At Easter in 1899 Eugenio Pacelli became Father Pacelli. He had earned his doctor's degrees. He was ordained and the day after this ceremony he celebrated his first Mass in the Chapel Borghese of St. Mary Major, at the bronze and lapis lazuli altar honoring the Madonna of the Snow.

His family were all at the April ceremony and there was the usual conjecture as to what would come next in Eugenio's career. His brother Francesco was following in the steps of their lawyer uncle Ernesto Pacelli, then called the third king of Rome. (As founder of the rich Banco di Roma and the first great Italian cinema organization, only Pope Leone and King Umberto were supposed to be more important.)

Father Pacelli was more sympathetically inclined to his uncle Vincenzo, a painter, who had encouraged him to study under the great art teacher Castelli. It was also Vincenzo Pacelli who backed the young priest in his love of the violin which he practiced constantly.

One day in that spring fifty years ago, as the young priest practiced his music, a visitor from the Vatican was announced. Eugenio rushed to meet the man, certain that he was to have an assignment.

Monsignor Gasparri, Secretary of Extraordinary Ecclesiastical Affairs in the Vatican Secretariat of State, had come in search of a young assistant. As the story goes, the stocky, mountain-bred Monsignor was brusque and harsh as he made his offer to the young priest. Although Pacelli's recommendations in the Vatican were of the highest, he looked frail *and* he played a violin.

Father Pacelli reluctantly accepted. "Actually I had not thought of administration. I hoped to dedicate myself to the care of souls."

At that, Gasparri is said to have answered, "I see. You want to become a shepherd. I will, instead, teach you how to be a good shepherd dog. You will learn to show your teeth."

As a protégé of Gasparri who later became Cardinal Secretary of State, Father Pacelli went up the ladder of Vatican diplomacy, using his obvious talents for writing and languages to the benefit of progressive international policies for his Church. He was apprentice at first, much later a subsecretary for the Congregation of Ecclesiastical Affairs. In 1917, before the outbreak of World War I, he was made Monsignor and Apostolic Nuncio to Berlin. During his twelve difficult years in Germany he earned the tribute *"Non nuntius sed angelus"* (not a nuncio but an angel).

Pius XI bestowed the red hat on Eugenio Pacelli in 1929 and made his family *marchesi.* In 1930, Cardinal Pacelli replaced Cardinal Gasparri as Secretary of State. His career was swiftly paced. He signed church treaties with Romania, Yugoslavia, Austria and the German Reich. He had twice officially visited England; he became delegate to the Eucharistic Congress in France, to another in Budapest. In 1934, he visited Buenos Aires, Montevideo, Rio de Janeiro, as the aging Pope's personal representative. When he returned from touring the United States and a visit to President Roosevelt in 1936, he was regarded as a probable successor to Pius XI. During the last years of his life Pius XI made constant and continual references to the qualifications of his dear cardinal for elevation—references solemnly heeded on March 2, 1949, when Eugenio Pacelli was elected Pius XII.

No cameras allowed in St. Peter's—they must be checked at the front door

"And ye shall hallow the fiftieth year and proclaim liberty throughout all the land unto all the inhabitants thereof; it shall be a jubilee unto you."

On Christmas Eve, the twenty-fifth Holy Year (1949-50 the first to be proclaimed by Pius XII) will be formally opened in a great ceremony at St. Peter's Church in Rome. Just as the *anno santo* was initiated 650 years ago in the days of Constantine, Pius XII will open the blocked-up holy door. Singing the versicle, "Open unto me the gates of justice," he will knock three times with a small silver hammer. The masonry which has been loosened beforehand is made to fall in at the third blow. When the threshold is swept clean by jubilee penitents, the Holy Father enters the church and the rites begin.

Ambassadors, delegates and important personages will be present. The famous a capella Sistine Choir will sing as the crimson-and-ermine-robed cardinals assist the Pope at the special Mass. The little bar in the sacristy will be opened and provisioned to refresh the dignitaries on hand.

Because the Pope and cardinals are never young men when the honor comes to them, a special retiring room has been built into the basilica. Here,

Exterior of the Holy Door in St. Peter's basilica. It has been plastered shut since the end of the Holy Year, 1933

A workman polishes the cross on the inside of the Holy Door. Pope Pius XII will reopen it Christmas Eve, 1949

During High Mass—sunlight streams down on the patterned marble floor of St. Peter's Church

Photograph originally taken for Look Magazine

the Holy Father may have a short rest and return to his throne before he is ever missed by the crowds that fill the six-acre church.

In the twelve months the holy door of St. Peter's (and the other basilicas St. John Lateran, St. Mary Major and St. Paul Outside the Wall) are open, hundreds of thousands of pilgrims from all over the world will pass through them seeking special indulgences of temporal punishment for sins.

Whether they make the prescribed fifteen or thirty visits—at High Mass or during the quiet of a rainy day when the pilgrims out are few—they will never fail to see and feel something new in St. Peter's.

The present church, built in the 120 years between 1506, when the architect Bramante turned in his completed plans and blueprints, and 1626, when it was finally dedicated by Urban VIII, is the largest Christian church in the world.

Begun by Bramante, for a while supervised by Raphael, with the glorious dome contributed by Michelangelo—the basilica of St. Peter's dominates the whole of the world's tiniest state.

One hundred thousand people can worship in St. Peter's at once. It is almost an eighth of a mile from the entrance down to the apse where the original wooden chair of St. Peter has been built into a gold and ivory altar. Every detail, however huge, is harmonious.

The plaster angels holding up the holy water font at the entrance are seven feet high, very big for cherubs. But as they are mounted against a pillar more than 100 feet in circumference the total effect is one of perfect proportion.

Other statues in the basilica are oversized too. In their niches high above the visitors' heads are fifteen-foot marble statues of founders of various religious orders. One of the problems now facing St. Peter's officials is what to do with the statues of other founding fathers now that the thirty-eighth and last place has been filled.

The surfaces of the interior are covered with mosaics of rare colored marbles and enamels; the 400-foot dome is one vast gold mosaic banded with a great frieze. On the frieze running around transepts and dome it is written in five-foot letters: "Thou are Peter and upon this rock I will build my Church; and to thee I will give the Keys of the Kingdom of Heaven. . . ."

Diffused and changing light streams down from the 290 windows set high in the great cupola or the ten smaller surrounding ones. The soft sunlight mutes the marbles and tiles, glances off the old mosaics to shimmer on the altar pieces and the polished prayer benches. His Excellency, Monsignor Ludovico Kaas, Economo of the basilica, says that every corner has its hour —at one time or another during the day, a shaft of light pierces the gloom around some treasure of the church, makes it for a brief moment more glorious than the others.

The "Pietà" may not be Michelangelo's greatest work but it rivals the sculptor's "Moses" and "David" for delicacy, outclasses them completely for harmony and spirit. The Virgin is very young-looking; the Son is broken and lifeless across her knees. It is badly placed against an unsympathetic background; it is almost too high to read the signature of Michelangelo on Our Lady's girdle—but these drawbacks do not seem to matter. All who see the "Pietà" are stilled and made sad by the moving quality of its beauty.

Many tourists believe at first glance that the old altarpieces are paintings, but there is only one oil in the entire church. Cortona's "Holy Trinity" hangs in the Chapel of the Blessed Sacrament where communion is given each morning. All the others are the products of the artists of the mosaic factory which has been fashioning them for more than three centuries.

No one should miss seeing these three mosaics—the "Navicella"—Peter walking on the waves to Christ—from Giotto; "The Last Communion of St. Jerome" from Dominichino; "The Transfiguration" from Raphael, with a self-portrait of the artist in a yellow robe gazing at Marina in pink. Marina was the young Raphael's love and in this great picture, not quite complete at his death, she has distracted his attention from the demented boy on whom the other figures concentrate.

There are days and days to be spent in St. Peter's with profit to the eyes and heart. The pilgrim there may confess in six or more languages, pray in twenty-seven different chapels. He can donate to St. Peter's Pence, kiss the foot of the venerated bronze statue of the saint, visit the crypts which will be really opened in 1950 for the first time in thirty years.

As it is customary for the cardinals created by each pope to supply a

proper monument after his death, a pilgrim may guess which popes were generous with the handing out of red hats. The monuments in the church tell the story. Some are richly impressive; others simple marble pieces. There are a few so extremely ugly that by no stretch of the imagination could they be called art.

The papal altar directly beneath the dome is made of a single block of marble from the ancient forum of Nerva. Here in the week before Easter, some of the most colorful of church ceremonies take place. Under the bronze Bernini canopy, the cardinals in their Lenten lavender (worn as mourning) clean the altar with rushes and oil. The Cardinal Grand Penitentiary sits in his throne near the pillar of Veronica; in his hand he holds a long wand with which he is privileged to touch those at prayer who seem particularly pious.

The celebrated ancient bronze statue of St. Peter, first bishop of Rome

Worn smooth by the kisses of thousands, the foot is saluted once more

Photograph originally taken for Look Magazine

The Penitentiaries of St. Peter's
hear confessions in French,
English, German, Italian,
Spanish or Portuguese as well
as in many other languages

An ancient coffer where the
conventional contribution of a
penny to St. Peter's Pence is
made on his birthday and
on special anniversaries

Canova's marble monument to
Clement XIII. The lion of
Religion bares his teeth at the
docile beast snoozing near
the young angel of Death

Three nuns reverently visit the basilica of St. Peter

Special indulgences are awarded for humility.

Almost any day, groups of starched little girls in white or a bevy of novices under the wing of an older nun can be seen kneeling at the Confession, the grave of St. Peter. There the pilgrims sing one of the reverent three-part chants to honor the saint.

About the Confession eighty-nine votive lamps burn continuously, except on Good Friday when they are dark. The lamps are now substitute bronze to replace the original silver ones stolen by Napoleon Bonaparte in a time of need.

At this spot, on July 29—the Feast Day of St. Peter—the Pope prays

The "Pietà." Michelangelo signed his name on the girdle of Our Lady

43

alone. Tradition has always demanded that this ceremony be private and at night by candlelight.

Behind a small grill set into the wall at this place, the *palliums*, honorary neckbands given by the Holy Father to archbishops and patriarchs for wear on high occasions are kept. Woven from the pure white wool of young lambs especially blessed before spring shearing, the *palliums* are coveted badges of honor.

Beneath the grill, extending as a deep well far down into the church crypts is the supposed tomb of Peter, first Bishop of Rome. Invisible for three centuries (the area has not been unsealed since the last recorded official investigation), the tomb or sarcophagus is currently the theme of much conjecture. There are a handful of men, including Pius XII, who know now whether the tomb has been found, whether it has been found empty or not, and what the chances are for positive proof of Peter's bones being Peter's bones.

An announcement is expected sometime at the beginning of the Holy Year 1949-50. Until then anybody's guess is good.

Archeological work in the oldest burial ground in Christendom, where lie the great of the Church through the ages, will add to history. Recent discoveries include dozens of pagan and Christian tombs two stories below the floor of the present basilica. These tombs lay along an ancient Roman road that wound up Vatican Hill. Near them has been found a little house, preserved even to a roof terrace, old broken statues and coins of Egyptian origin.

Here in the grotto is the tomb of Pius XI who, because he wished to be placed in death near the man he loved in life—Pius X, indirectly started the digging. Monsignor Kaas was directing workmen in the removal of a marble slab next to the tomb of Pius X when the entire wall fell out and revealed a crypt of some size behind.

Systematic investigations followed. Hollow walls were found by tapping—mapped—excavated. Evidences of the two old churches to honor Peter were actually found. The whole area has been greatly extended.

In the crypts, the Spanish Cardinal Merry del Val—close friend of Pope Pius XII for many years—lies next to the last of the English Stuarts. The heart of Christine of Sweden is kept in a beautiful urn; the only English pope, Nicholas Breakspeare, is at rest in a huge red granite tomb. The popularity of the crypts as burial places shows the common desire of Christians to be close in death to the church and its founder.

It is possible to ride up to the roof. But it is more amusing to walk, for along the circular stairway winding up to the dome of St. Peter's, marble slabs testify to the prowess (or lack of it) in royalty. The young Shah of Persia, in the company of Count Enrico Galeazzi, made it all the way to the top some years ago. King Alphonso of Spain, Carlotta and Maximilian of Mexico, gave up midway. So did Frederick of Prussia.

The first roof of St. Peter's is not at all like the usual roof. It wanders uphill and down, around the smaller domes in the shadow of the great one Michelangelo worked to perfect the last eighteen years of his life. There are shops, a post office, a photographer's studio and the workrooms of the San Pietrini (St. Peter's workmen).

From the front balustrade beneath the feet of the huge saints' statues, there is a wonderful view of St. Peter's Square and the long curved arms of

An ancient Roman crypt with classic tombs—part of recent discoveries made during excavations far below the main floor of St. Peter's basilica

INGRESSO ALLA CUPOLA
ENTRÉE À LA COUPOLE
ENTRANCE TO THE CUPOLA
EINGANG ZUR KUPPEL
ENTRADA A LA CÚPULA
ENTRADA À CUPOLA
WEJŚCIE NA KOPUŁĘ

the two Bernini colonnades.

Slightly higher than the roof there is a gallery running like a ribbon around the inside of the mosaic dome. Whispers into the mosaic wall carry as clearly as bell tones across the distance of 138 feet, so perfect are the acoustics. From this point the interior of the cathedral seems bathed in luminous light; it is a glorious and heady thing to see.

At the very top balcony reached by a slanted staircase running between the outside supporting drum and the dome itself, there are all the views of the Vatican—and Rome as well.

East: St. Peter's Square and the wide Via del Conciliazione running down to the Tiber. Beyond are the seven hills of ancient Rome, the Pantheon dome gleaming in the late afternoon sun, the Quirinal Palace, the wedding-cake monument to King Victor Emmanuel and the towers of the basilica of St. Mary Major.

North: the great Vatican palace honeycombed with passages, stairways, courtyards—beyond it running above head level is the famous *passetto*, a tunnel in mid-air, used by the popes as an escape hatch to the Castel Sant' Angelo when trouble threatened.

West: the governor's marble palace, the railway station, the Ethiopian

Visitors wander among the small cupolas which dot the roof of St. Peter's

On the front roof of St. Peter's Church, 19-foot statues of Christ and His Apostles (except St. Peter) stand guard over the Piazza below

College—all the 108 acres of the Vatican and the Vatican gardens. From this point one may sometimes see the Holy Father taking his late afternoon walk—a slender figure in white pacing a green path behind the Radio Station.

South: the extraterritorial properties of the Vatican, the College of Propaganda, the line of statues atop the basilica of St. John Lateran, the Colosseum. Beyond the church spires of Rome and away to the south and west lies the blue Mediterranean, clearly visible on good days.

A rare view of the church steps and entrance from Monsignor Montini's terrace

Photograph originally taken for Look Magazine

Map of the Vatican

1 Museums
2 Libraries
3 Entrance to Museums, Libraries
4 Pinacoteca—Art Gallery
5 Old Gardens
6 New Gardens of Pius XI
7 Old Observatory
8 Ethiopian College
9 Radio Station HVJ
10 Vatican Sports Field
11 Railroad Station
12 Mosaic Factory
13 Governor's Palace
14 Tapestry Workshop
15 Electric Power Plant
16 Summer Villa of Pius IV
17 Belvedere Courtyard
18 Marshals' Court
19 Borgia Court
20 Parrots' Court
21 Courtyard of St. Damascus
22 Papal Palace, Residence of Pius XII
23 Sistine Chapel
24 Basilica of St. Peter
25 The Bronze Door
26 Gate of the Bells
27 Post Office
28 Newspaper and Printing Shop
29 Apartment House for Citizens
30 The Annona
31 Gate of St. Anna
32 Swiss Guards Barracks
33 St. Peter's Square
34 Sacristy

On four following pages—views of the
Holy City from the cupola of St. Peter's Church

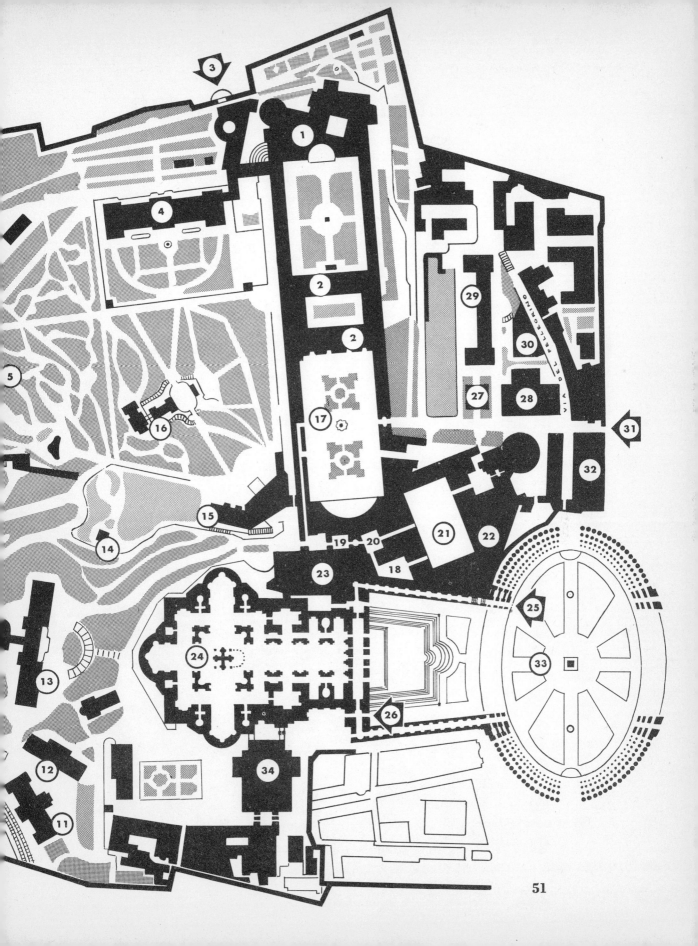

East

South

21 Courtyard of St. Damascus   **22** Papal Palace, Residence of Pius XII   **23** Sistine Chapel

24 Basilica of St. Peter   **33** St. Peter's Square   **34** Sacristy

Southwest

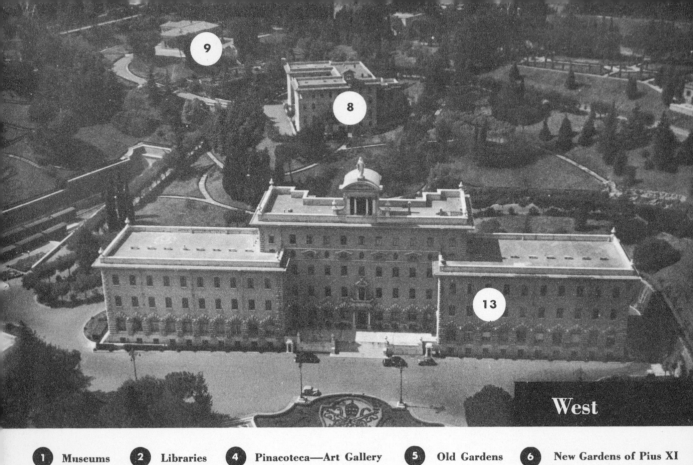

West

North

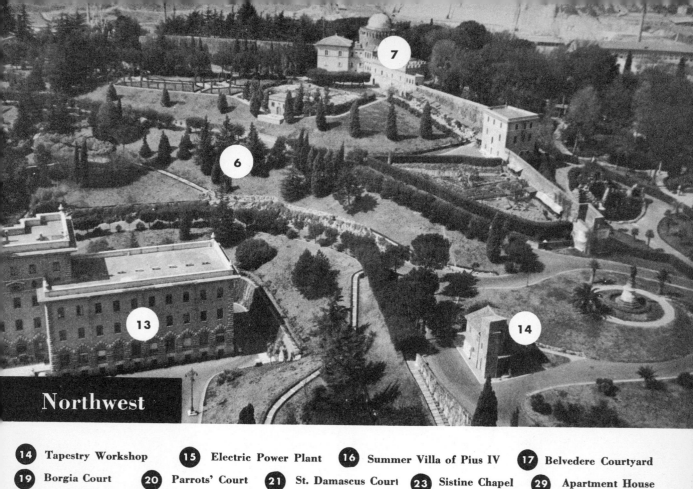

Northwest

Northeast

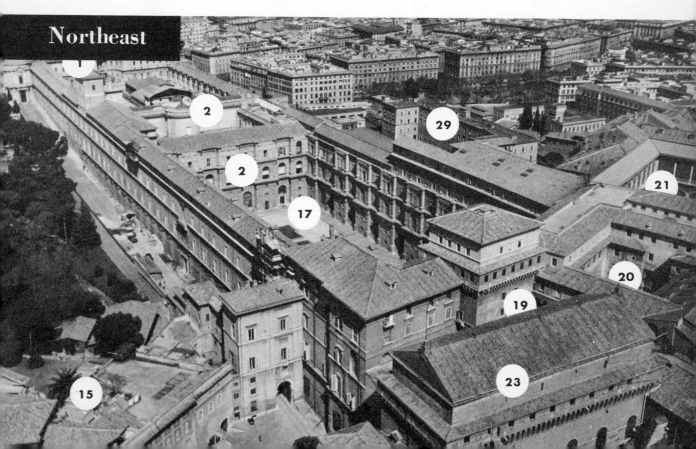

The Treasures

Books and paintings and statues are timeless. They are the currency of ideas and ideals and, as such, have been "coin of the realm" of the Vatican and the popes for many lifetimes.

Beyond price, the Vatican collections are one of the riches of the Holy City. The Church's patronage of the arts has declined in recent centuries—there are no Monets, Manets, Picassos or Renoirs or pieces of Carl Milles to be found in the museums—but reverence for what it has is high. And should one of the current lively and great artists turn again to work for the Church, it is likely that he would find a place in Vatican collections or a proctor among Vatican personnel. Daily, in the Bramante-designed, Raphael-decorated private reception room of the Secretariat of State, there appear young artists and authors who have work to show; they are always seen and it is known that they receive encouragement from high officials.

Perhaps for the reason that art—in architecture, metal work, murals and mosaics—is everywhere one looks in the Holy City, everyone in the place is interested in it. A lawyer of the Sacra Rota who is a Raphael enthusiast last year made an amazing art discovery which will ultimately add to Vatican prestige. In a small junk or second-hand store in Rome, Avocato Leccesi found and bought a complete and the only known set of the Volpato miniature engravings of Raphael's loggia. The importance of this find was two-fold. Wind and rain in the two centuries the loggia was left open to weather ruined

In the Raphael rooms, scaffolding hides the frescos now being repaired

the walls of this frescoed corridor in the palace. The ceiling with its fifty-two panels of the so-called Raphael Bible suffered slightly less, but an itinerant artist at some time in the past "restored" those—garishly, badly. The Volpatos are in color, are absolutely faithful and delightful reproductions of the walls and ceilings as they looked when first done. Although this collection has not been seen by more than a dozen people as yet, it is hoped that sometime during the Holy Year it will be exhibited by the fortunate owner.

The charming and gifted Raphael, called divine by many, was an architect, silversmith, wood carver, oil and mural painter. His partially obliterated murals in the loggia had a humor and delicacy found in none of his other works, but it is the murals in the Raphael *stanze* (rooms) which were a four-year labor of the artist for Julius II that best show his mastery.

"The Disputa," a glorification of "The Blessed Sacrament" and "The School of Athens," which contains a self-portrait of the artist in the right corner and a portrait of Michelangelo in the left, are the three most famed of the ceiling to floor murals. It is estimated that as many as fifty of Raphael's pupils worked with him on this extensive job. The recorded price, large for those days, was about $2800.

Hundreds of years have left their mark on these treasures too. They are riddled with cracks and the top layer of plaster is loose from the wall in many large areas. In the early part of 1949, the project to repair the cracks and prevent any pieces falling completely away to the floor was started. Prefect of the museums Baron Nogara estimates that it will take seven years to do the delicate "doctoring" necessary to preserve the frescos. When the casein injections have been finished and the paintings pronounced restored, they will be ready for another two hundred years of tourists.

In the Pinacoteca, the three masterpieces of Raphael have a splendid room to themselves. "The Coronation of Our Lady," painted at the age of twenty before he came to Rome; the beautiful "Madonna of Foligno," which came to the Vatican only after it was rescued from the French on the fall of Napoleon, and the great "Transfiguration," which was not quite finished when Raphael died on Good Friday in 1520, are not for sale but their estimated value exceeds $3,000,000.

Of the greatest Gobelin tapestries in the Vatican, one set is the scenes

Casein injections are given the Raphael murals in the Vatican Museum

from the Acts of the Apostles designed by Raphael and his pupils, executed in silk and gold and colors by the great weaver, Peter van Aelst of Brussels. The ten tapestries, each 15 by 130 feet, were designed to cover the lower walls of the Sistine Chapel. Shortly after they were finished and hung, they were stolen. Later returned, they were stolen again. The glass cases in which they are presently exhibited are locked and guarded.

In the Hall of the Tapestries, the Gobelin of "The Last Supper" designed and fashioned under the direction of Leonardo da Vinci has been painstakingly mended and returned to the wall along with those of an exquisite set portraying the Life of Christ.

The Pinacoteca galleries house the work of hundreds of artists, most of it on religious subjects. Raphael's teacher, Perugino, Melozzo da Forli, Pinturicchio, Giovanni Santi, Raphael's father—Leonardo da Vinci—Titian—Paul Veronese—Murillo of the madonnas—Domeninchino and Giotto are the best known names signed to the magnificent paintings that line the rooms.

There is little of the sweet Fra Angelico's work in the galleries, but the gem of Vatican chapels, known as The Chapel of Nicolas V, is almost all frescos by the saintly friar from Florence. Recently this very small room has been stripped and restored to the fresh loveliness of the fifteenth century. It will be opened to visitors during the Holy Year.

Perhaps the most grandiose exhibition of art is the Sistine Chapel; it is all art. And it is for the most part the work of the titan Michelangelo. Botticelli, Perugino and other pre-Raphaelites painted some of the lesser frescos below the windows, but the great end wall behind the altar is thousands of square feet of vigorous, moving Michelangelo. This fresco of "The Last Judgement" shows Christ as the judge of the world—sending the holy and the blessed on His right to Heaven, the damned on His left to Hell. During a celebration of the Mass in this dark chapel, the candles on the altar light the figures of the mural so they almost seem to move.

"The Last Judgement" was a solo effort of the artist at sixty; he devoted seven years to it and went on from it to work almost twenty-five years completing the basilica of St. Peter's and designing and building the great dome.

The frescoed vaulted ceiling of the Sistine Chapel was done by Michelangelo when he was a much younger and more athletic man. High on scaffold-

In the Pinacoteca—a miniature painter copies a Raphael Madonna

ing built especially to accommodate him, several patient trusted pupils and beds for all, the artist lived for almost five years. Blinded occasionally with falling plaster, harassed at every turn by an impatient pontiff who wanted to push the undertaking through and exhibit his prize, Michelangelo lay on his back day after day and filled the vast arched ceiling—with its holes, corners, irregular planes—with literally hundreds of figures.

This work showing the Creation of Man, the Flood and the Fall of Man was—is—a daring artistic concept and a fantastic use of all available space. The figures on the ceiling are depicted in an amazing variety of positions. Each one was foreshortened and painted with the greatest art and skill so that the space is filled and the result is a marvelous example of the artist's mastery of perspective.

In the first field, the Almighty separates Light from Darkness. The Sun and the Moon are created and the Earth brings forth plants and herbs in the second.

Fish are created to live in the waters. Adam is made and joined by the creature woman. In the sixth field, Satan appears as the essence of evil in a snake's form. Adam and Eve eat of the forbidden fruit and are expelled from Heaven; the floods float Noah's ark into the raging water.

Recently cleaned and checked for needed repair, the ceiling is in ex-

Italian students in the Sistine Chapel crane their necks to look at the murals high on the ceiling above them. Painted by Michelangelo between 1509 and 1512, they show the Creation and Fall of Man from grace, the Deluge

Michelangelo painted the magnificently detailed Sistine ceiling lying on his back on a very high platform built for the project

terwards, he modestly wrote of his labors: "False and
aint I know must be the fruit of squinting eye and brain"

cellent condition. Crick in the neck notwithstanding, it takes hours of patient craning to properly see and appreciate the caravan of movement and color in the Sistine.

A great deal of the repair, refurbishing and cleaning or conservation work for which the Vatican has an enviable reputation is done on the location. Anything that can be moved—and this includes the entire frescos of walls of the Sala Chiaroscuri—is restored in the large repair shops beneath the Pinacoteca.

The "clinic" runs classes for experts from other countries at stated intervals during the year. In these classes, Vatican techniques, discovered by the advanced and expert workmen in the clinic, are taught. Rotten wooden backings for oils are carefully scaled off and at the right juncture the layer of dried oil paint that is the masterpiece is scaled off in the opposite direction having been glued face flat to clean canvas.

Eventually, as in the case of Raphael's "Madonna of Foligno," several Giottos and the famed Leonardo da Vinci of "St. Jerome," all is new except the ancient picture. Mounted on rot-proofed, worm-proof wood braced trickily against warping, the pictures are in better condition than when new. Dry-cleaning of age-dirtied canvases is successfully done in this laboratory which also serves as the clearing house for complete documentation of art for the archives. Photographs in detail are made of all the pieces for future reference.

The laboratory where the nuns painstakingly mend precious tapestries with sun-faded silk threads, renew the delicate embroideries of precious state robes or altar cloths, the mosaic factory for repairs and new art works and the manuscript clinic for books complete the picture of Vatican ingenuity in caring for what they have. The manuscript clinic has produced several new methods of arresting book decay and removing the dirt and fungus that sometimes attacks invaluable manuscripts.

The basilica of St. Peter, like the libraries and museums, is a vast storehouse of Vatican art. The statuary of tombs and saints is second in importance to the mosaics above the altars and the mosaic-lined dome. This art, at its peak, resulted in the founding of the Mosaic Studio in the Vatican. Established in 1576, the studio's first and greatest commission was the decoration

In St. Peter's—a mosaic reproduction of Raphael's great "Transfiguration"

of St. Peter's dome and the making of the altar panels such as the "Transfiguration" and the "Last Confession of St. Jerome."

Housed in a small modern "factory" built by Pius XI next the railway station behind the church, the plant takes orders for church decoration from all over the world. In the summer of 1949 after two years of work, they finished a second "Transfiguration" from Raphael which, mounted and crated, finally went off to a large Chicago church.

The artists of the studio have come for many centuries from the same families. The particular and delicate skills required for this work seem to be hereditary. Sons of mosaic artists come in to work as young as eight. After hours, in free time from art school, they run errands and keep sparkling clean the collection of madonnas, saints and flower mosaics on sale in the roomy front halls of the studio. By the age of ten the children graduate to final polishing and cleaning of finished work; they are also permitted to knead the dark rubbery gutta-percha plaster into which the mosaic bits are set.

The stockroom of the mosaic factory is made up of endless rows of steel cabinets. There are 27,000 drawers and each compartment contains fragments of one particular color or shade of a color—in marbles, made enamels, jasper, stone. Many of the materials are secretly manufactured in the studio and the lovely Cardinal red and Madonna blue tints in enamels have never been duplicated elsewhere.

An artist begins by drawing a cartoon or *dessin* in the actual size of his finished mosaic. This tissue is fastened on a board covered with plaster; the artist then traces the outlines of a part of the cartoon into the plaster, removes the tissue, and adds fresh wet gutta-percha or stucco to the area he will first work.

A large piece of enamel is broken with a hammer, chipped down until it is the correct shape and set into the stucco, which when slowly and completely dried will stay fixed for a thousand years. Colors are faded or blended over lamp flames, aligned and set into the base with tweezers and mallet. Records kept in the mosaic factory show that as many as half of the 27,000 varying shades and hues have met in one great panel.

The products of this studio, now scattered to the farthest territories of the Roman Catholic Church's communicants, are a great pride of the Vatican.

Artists in the Mosaic Studio work to produce another "Transfiguration"

"Everyone can have something of the Holy City where they are," the director, Monsignor Kaas, once said. "And it seems that everyone does want it. We are getting increasingly distant orders to fulfill."

No visit to the Holy City treasures would be finished without looking into the Treasury and Sacristy of St. Peter's Church where among the church jewels and the tiara and robes of St. Peter's statue are kept the relics. Only occasionally exposed—and then for veneration—these include two Thorns of the Savior's crown and another fragment of the True Cross which the Emperor Constantine always carried on his person in a gold box (one is mounted in the cross on top of the obelisk in St. Peter's Square).

The first tour of the other Vatican museums—Greek, Etruscan, Egyptian —is sometimes confusing. The rooms are overcrowded, notwithstanding the fact that much of little value has been stored elsewhere. Many of the pieces are second-rate copies. Actually their chief value is historical record of great periods, and if the alert art enthusiast sorts out what he wishes to see, his reward is more than aching legs.

The Etruscan Museum has rather good things discovered during the years near Rome. Included are the treasures of the Regolini-Galasini tomb (with the three-wheeled warrior's chariot in running order) discovered near Cerveteri in 1836. The Egyptian Rooms boast the miniature statue of the priest Naophorus from the sixth century before Christ and the usual lot of mummies, trinkets and jewels. They are interesting to young students and history readers.

The most important section in the museums is devoted to Greek art and houses the extensive collections of marbles. "The Belvedere Torso," supposedly done by Apollonius while staying in Rome shortly after the death of St. Peter, is considered one of the finest pieces; the "Laocoön" group, complete with writhing snakes and discovered in the palace of Titus in 1506 was the beginning of the Vatican Museum as such; a copy of the Myron discus-thrower looking, as always, in the wrong direction, is interesting.

A basin from the hot baths of Titus, a Jupiter bust, the young gymnast and his slave, the Greek boy with his goose, the disputed Apollo with a bow, the sacrifice of Mithra, the bull, and the monumental Nile group with the fertile god amiably permitting sixteen small children to climb over him

Thousands of tiny stone chips and enamels are inlaid in one colorful mosaic

70

(the Nile in flood rises 16 cubits), are good to see if the visitor remembers that their importance is scarcely as original and rare and unique works of art—but rather that they were found in and about Rome and, as originals or copies, indicate something of the wealth of the past and the passing of a period in Vatican history.

Both for casual lookers and students, the beautiful Map Hall and the Hall of the Animals with its lions, eagles, horses, cows and pigs that once stood in the gardens of luxurious Roman villas are worth hours. They picture amusingly and actually what was.

There are five Vatican libraries—and although one usually associates the word "library" with many-volumed shelves, three of the five are completely bare of books. They are the Sistine Library, built by Sixtus, the Library of Inscriptions and the Numismatic Library.

The Sistine is the place of display of the precious Sèvres vases, jewels and gifts which popes through the ages have received from friendly royalty. Beautifully vaulted and frescoed, these great halls are in the transverse wing of the great Belvedere Palace and their windows give on the formal court below where the guards can be seen in mid-morning at gun drill. No books show. What still remain in the rooms are old manuscripts and early account books of papal finances—and these are hidden behind the locked doors of lovely old painted cabinets.

Any of the old employees seen about the place is approachable and will, with interest, explain the stories of the alphabet originators, writers, early libraries and historic Vatican occasions painted on the walls. The custodians will also unlock a cabinet and allow a visitor to see how carefully funds were collected, registered, and dispersed many hundreds of years ago when the Constantine basilica was built on the present location of St. Peter's. They are better than any paid guide or a guidebook because of their overwhelming pride in their occupation—and most of them have been where they are for so long that the Farnese clock given to Leo XIII and the gold-crested china seem part theirs. Unconsciously, they use "we" when recounting the Colonna burning of papal books, the story of the moving of the great obelisk in the Piazza or the tale of how Constantine the Emperor officiated at the excavation for the new church and himself carried away twelve

Framed in a sunny window, the Vatican's statue of the discus thrower

baskets of earth to honor the twelve apostles.

The Stone Museum, commonly known as the Library of Inscriptions, also contains neither books nor manuscripts. Here are to be found more than three thousand marble and brick slabs, tablets and pieces of tablets covered with Latin writing. There are the rolls of honor much as are found today in town squares as memorials to war dead. In lieu of the trappings and devices of modern advertising methods, the Romans put up marble slabs. One of these, touting a Roman bath outside the city, is displayed with the following translation of its message affixed below: "Visit our establishment. Under new management. All the newest improvements and ultra-modern comforts. Reasonable rates too!"

The graphites of terra cotta, with inscriptions inexpertly scratched under the sign of the cross or the fish, are valuable as early documents of Christian persecution. Many like them—reading "God care for you" or "Rest in peace" or "Pray for us left behind"—are set into the dank stair wells and corridors of the catacombs near the city. To the philosophic reader they are interesting contrast to the inscribed farewells of the pagans with their "goodbye forever" resignation.

The Numismatic Library with its extensive collection of coins and medals holds a record so far unbeaten by other Vatican libraries—that of the young man aged thirteen who came to Rome for a three weeks' visit and spent seventeen days of his tour sightseeing in this one spot.

There are here almost 100,000 pieces including most of the coins issued by the Papal Mint since the sixth century. This library holds the especial interest of the governor of the Vatican, Marquis Serafini, who is an acknowledged expert in collections of stamps and coins.

The Pontifical Archives under the supervision of Monsignor Angelo Mercati, brother of the Prefect Giovanni Cardinal Mercati, are a collection of 85,000 folio volumes and string-tied bundles which contain the historical letters, contracts, treaties, papal bulls, registers, petitions and pacts of the Vatican. For value, amusement and as a source of original research, they are unequaled anywhere in the world. Here is church history complete—and the history of some European countries' privy affairs from day to day as reported by priests and nuncios from the fourth century until recently.

Schoolgirls cluster about a replica of St. Stephen's crown. The original
was sent by Cardinal Mindszenty, before his imprisonment, from Hungary to
the safety of the American officials in the U.S. Zone of Germany

These archives do not deserve the usual designation of secret archives. Admittedly some of the more recent reports and communications of the Sacred Congregations and the Secretariat of State are withheld—but what is on hand is there for scholars to consult. And scholars from every country and every religion do work from these papers. They may read the petition from English churchmen urging the Pope to annul the marriage of Henry the Eighth to Catharine of Aragon (which was denied), trace a fifteenth-century quarrel with the Medicis of Florence, or consult the files that will register their Ph.D. thesis on court life before the fall of Constantinople as superior. There is nothing ancient about the cross-index used in the archives or the amazing and facile arrangement of the papers; experts have spent years putting them in order.

Most important of all the libraries is *the* Vatican Library. The pride of its learned bibliophile prefect, Cardinal Mercati, this library was reorganized and modernized by Pius XI, who as Cardinal Ratti had been in charge of the famed Ambrosian Library in Milan as well as Mercati's predecessor at the Vatican Library.

Although Pius XI kept the library running on a shoestring ($10,000 an-

In the vaulted Vatican Library, modernized by Pius XI, there are U.S. steel shelves, an air-control system and the newest in cross-file book systems

Students, researchers and writers from all over the world are permitted to use manuscripts and books from Vatican collections

The Sistine Library is a showplace for murals and the gifts to popes

nually approved as a budget), he was extremely generous and free-handed in assigning large sums to special projects. He had a New Jersey firm install steel shelves, and special heating and ventilating units were built in so that temperature and humidity could be controlled. For months, the delicate maneuvers of electricians putting in the excellent lighting system without harm to the painted walls and panels were the concern of all the employees. The system of book cataloguing and classification now used were borrowed with permission from the United States Library of Congress.

To make modernization complete, the genial Pius XI even conceded that women might be students, and today the collection of 70,000 manuscripts, half a million printed books and 7,500 incunabula (early rough-printed

Behind doors of the painted cabinets, old papers and accounts are kept

books) are available and used by nuns, college girls and women of the world who write, research, and teach.

Unlike Topsy in *Uncle Tom's Cabin* or a famous modern university library where purchases and inheritances are frequent, the Vatican Library did not "just grow." As early as the Middle Ages, there was a library of the popes from which books could be borrowed—small, but probably the first of public libraries. Some of these books were lost, others not returned. Some were pillaged or destroyed in wars—or even, as in the case of the Colonna story, purposefully burned as an insult. (The story has modern consequences, so the Romans say. Because, in the fourteenth century, an early member of the Colonna family deliberately destroyed the manuscripts of Boniface VIII in a fit of rage, the Colonna Palace still shakes on its foundations on the anniversary of this occurrence.)

By the time of Nicolas V, Sixtus IV and Sixtus V, the Medicis in Florence were so successfully collecting manuscripts, including rare writings from the Far East, that the fever and wish to do likewise caught in the Vatican. Scholars were sent out on searches; lines for donations were laid. By the time Maximilian of Bavaria had enriched the collections by the contents of the *Bibliotheca Palatina* of Heidelberg, when that town was taken in the Thirty Years' War, the value of the books was realized, and the strictest control was exercised over their borrowing and use.

There is no assessed value to the books and manuscripts in the Vatican, but there are some rare pieces handled only by Cardinal Mercati. If at all possible, a Vatican visitor ought to see the notebooks and original scores of Palestrina, the greatest composer of church music; the thirteenth-century Old Testament which is the largest book in the world and kept in a case with the smallest which can be hidden in a fist; the fourth-century Old Testament in Greek called *the* Vatican codex and its greatest treasure.

In the Vatican Library—the Gutenberg Bible, first printed book in the world

Inside the Vatican

To ALMOST 350,000,000 PEOPLE the capital of the religious world is a miniature city-state of 108 acres lying in a half-circle behind St. Peter's Church in Rome. Here, in Vatican City, Pope Pius XII lives and works. From his historical palace, built layer-cake style on a hill by the Tiber River, he governs the vast congregation of the Holy Roman Catholic Church.

For two thousand years the slope of Vatican Hill has been the geographical center of the Church, but the Vatican state has existed as the world's smallest nation only twenty years. The signing of the Lateran Treaty, Concordat and Financial Accord on February 11, 1929, brought the state into being, settled the so-called Roman Question.

This historic quarrel began in 1870 when Victor Emmanuel II, King of Sardinia and Piedmont, seized Rome and the last of the papal territories which had once covered most of central Italy. Pope Pius IX retaliated by excommunicating the king and retired from his Quirinal Palace in Rome proper to the Vatican Palace, where he locked the gates and began his exile.

The king's ministers voted a million and a half dollars as an annual compensation to the Pope for loss of revenue from Rome and the rich surrounding Romagna countryside.

The money was ignored, never touched. For fifty-nine years neither side attempted a *rapprochement*. Old Italian noble families, remaining loyal to the papacy, locked their front doors, pulled their curtains and kept them

Swiss Guards with halberds stand in the innermost court of the old Vatican

pulled through the long years. Known as the "black" aristocracy, they refused to hold office in the royal government or to see, speak to, meet or marry with the "white" aristocracy of the invading nobility. Each of Rome's "rulers" did his best to ignore the existence of the other.

Not until the capable Achille Ratti moved from prefect of the Vatican libraries to become Pius XI was there real hope for a solution. The mild Pope from Lombardy in the north of Italy knew no other Vatican than the locked Vatican. But he had grown to manhood in a united Italy and it seemed to him the old quarrel should be settled once and for all. He found support in an unexpected quarter—Benito Mussolini, the king's first minister and creator of the Fascist state.

Pius XI made the first move by appearing on the central balcony of St. Peter's basilica for a public blessing. Mussolini recognized the departure for what it was meant to be and sent a minister from his Foreign Office to query the Vatican lawyer, Francesco Pacelli, brother of Monsignor Eugenio Pacelli.

The Vatican lawyer said that the Roman Question had one solution as far as the Vatican was concerned—a piece of land and a concordat agreeing to make religious marriages legal.

This first conversation took place in August, 1926. Nine hundred and twenty days later, the papers were public and legal. In that time Francesco Pacelli had held 110 conferences with Mussolini's ministers at the Foreign Office, 26 with Mussolini himself. He had sat through 64 unending *pourparlers* with Cardinal Secretary of State Gasparri, had been in 129 private and secret audiences with Pius XI. He had supervised the 21 rewritings necessary to make the treaty in all ways acceptable.

For all this delicate and long-winded diplomacy, the Vatican got the concordat legalizing marriages, a financial settlement, and a grant of a piece of land about the size of an 18-hole golf course or a decent-sized Kansas farm.

The Vatican state is exempt from Italian taxes and Italian laws. Although the great Square of St. Peter lying between the long curving arms of the Bernini colonnades is policed by Italian police as a safety courtesy gesture, it is papal territory.

Behind the gates—the five frontiers of the Vatican—neither Italians

Main Street in the Holy City—the Via Pelligrino or Pilgrim Street

#1 frontier of the Holy City—
a painted wooden barrier
and Swiss Guards halt the pedestrian
and cars at the Gate of the Bells

The Bronze Door through which
pilgrims go to an audience

nor any others may go without good reason and proper credentials or permissions.

Directly to the left of St. Peter's basilica is the Gate of the Bells which bears the heaviest traffic into the Holy City. Brilliantly clad Swiss Guards are always on duty here; halberds gleaming in the sun when the weather is good—half hidden in a small wooden guard house during the cold months. A black-and-white-striped barrier crosses the road under the archway and it is swung open for autos and pedestrians recognized or presenting the proper papers to the guards.

Behind the Gate of the Bells begins the "avenue" of the Vatican, the Via delle Fondemente, which circles the apse of the church of St. Peter to

The Museum entrance—tourists descend here daily by the busload to see the world-famous Vatican art collections

The back door of the Vatican—St. Anna Gate which is used as a service entrance and by Holy City citizens

the "old Vatican" where it passes under the walls of the Sistine Chapel, narrows to run through the Court of the Sentry, the Court of the Ancient Borgia Tower, the Parrot's Court (around which cluster offices of the crowded Secretariat of State), the Marshal's Court where visiting cardinals are housed during conclaves to elect a new Pope, and finally winds up in the great Court of St. Damascus. Around this last court is built the great three-winged palace of the popes. From the courtyard there is a great stair, and an elevator, leading up to the second-floor apartments of the Holy Father where audiences are held.

If one drives *through* the Vatican, one avoids all these narrow courts with the sharp turns and whips through the Belvedere Courtyard and directly out the Gate of St. Anna, having made a complete circle of the little state in less than five minutes' driving time.

As it leads directly into the little "village" of the Holy City, the Gate of St. Anna is really the Vatican back door, a kind of service and supply entrance. It is so clogged with citizen traffic—bicycles and pedestrians—that the guards stationed there are supposed to allow only cardinals and *camions* (trucks) out that way.

The most famous entrance to the Vatican, for pedestrians only, is the *Porto Bronzo,* the Bronze Door, located at the right of the façade of the basilica in the shade of the Bernini columns. This door is the entrance for the pedestrian pilgrims who happily come to trudge the long *Scala Pia* or *Scala Regia* stairs to the St. Damascus Court and a state audience with His Holiness. The Bronze Door is always guarded by the Swiss—two, four, or six at a time depending on expected traffic.

A fourth and most important frontier is the railway entrance to the Vatican. This "iron curtain," which is rolled back two or three times a week to allow in freight trains is located on the south wall of the Vatican and called the Fabbrica Gate. The Vatican station and tracks were built as a good-will gesture in 1931 by the Italian government; they cost more than six million lira at that date—most of which went into the miniature white marble station. The royal waiting room is a poem of white, green, yellow and pink pastel marbles stuck together with bronze filagree and rich decorations. It has never been used. No passenger has ever arrived or departed from the

Iron curtain of the Holy City—the Fabbrica Gate for freight trains only

Photograph originally taken for Look Magazine

station and the very fancy papal train which was built in 1858 was used on only one occasion before it was retired to the Museum of Rome.

The rail system itself is the shortest in existence. It consists of two tracks about 300 yards long, joined beyond the Urban Wall to the Italian main line. Freight trains back in; for loading and unloading they are shunted into an excavated hill as though they were Lionel toy trains. This rail facility is important to the Vatican. Because there are no customs or import-export duties to be paid, goods for church missions and personnel are ordered sent into the Holy City, and from there they are reshipped at considerable savings. There is a 60 per cent deduction on freight fares for building materials and varied other items over the Italian rails to the Vatican which means that most of the necessaries for churches all over Italy are sent to the Vatican and then trucked to the spot of construction.

A fifth way into the Vatican is a public entrance and leads from the Roman street running along the north wall directly into the Biblioteca (libraries) and Pinocoteca (painting and art galleries).

The Vatican acreage may be roughly divided in four—the public part including St. Peter's Church, the museums and libraries; the official, with buildings such as the governor's beautiful palace on the hill behind St. Peter's; the "village" clustered around the great 1000-room papal palace; the gardens which cover almost half the total space between the walls.

Pius XI is called the "building Pope" with reason; almost 50 per cent of what can be seen from the roof and balconies on the basilica is his work. The little spic-and-span three-cell jail was part of his program to make the Vatican almost self-sustaining. When the news got out in Rome that the Holy City was to have its own "prison," there was quite some commotion. Pius XI let it be known that he personally had inspected the place to be certain there were no instruments of torture and that provision had been made for a small exercise court, proper sanitation, and good beds.

Since not more than a dozen crimes have occurred in the Vatican in the past fifty years, the jail does not do a rushing business. Two workmen once pinched pennies from St. Peter's alms box in the basilica and were comfortably detained in the jail until the Vatican lower court could decide on proper punishment.

Gift of the Italian government—a pastel marble railway station

Mission supplies are shipped from the Vatican to points all over the globe

Another time when a madwoman shot down a priest in the basilica, the jail was used to house her only until the Italian police arrived to take her away. In the case of Chippico, a Monsignor demoted to just plain Signor, his rank and the nature of the crime ruled out a jail. As a result the offender was detained under guard in his apartments. When he escaped his Vatican guard, the Italian police found him and kept him. Crime is not a major problem in the world's smallest state.

The "village," lying just inside St. Anna Gate, is one place where a stranger could get lost without trouble. The modern and the old stand chock-a-block and there are too many small alleys and courts to make direction-finding simple. Along or very near Via Pellegrino (the Way of the Pilgrim) which is the village main street, are the telephone and telegraph offices, the pharmacy and first-aid clinic run by the Brothers of Charity, the central Vatican post office, and the Annona provision store. Also in the area

A Roman bathtub stands before the Vatican's oldest church—St. Stephen of the Abyssinians

The Holy City heat and power plant—a modern and important part of Pius XI's building program

are the large Vatican garages, barracks and canteens for the Swiss Guards, the nuns' tapestry repair studios, the citizens' apartment house, the workman's canteen, the government sanitation offices, the machine shops and the power plant.

The power plant, another of Pius XI's buildings, is slightly more grand than seems in keeping with its use. On the top floor giant turbines painted a deep Empire green are sunk at measured intervals in a marble floor. The walls up to head level are matching marble; on a balcony running along the wall switches and controls are sunk into a marble panel. There isn't a spot of grease or dirt in the place. With crucifixes and a portrait of the Pope on the wall, it appears to be almost anything save what it is.

On the floor below there is the great jet-fired, oil-burning heat system that warms the Vatican buildings. In the Holy Father's own apartments there is a secondary and smaller independent heating system.

The Vatican lock-up. This miniature three-cell jail is never full, is sometimes closed and empty

The Vatican fire department jeep—and firemen placing loudspeakers for an open-air ceremony

With all his efficiency in construction of the buildings in his domain, Pius XI's greatest enthusiasm was for the gardens; he added thirty-two acres of new landscaping during his years as Pope—doubling the area set aside to beauty.

You will never find the gardens of the Vatican in a listing of those that are historical or world-famous. They are smaller than the Villa Borghese gardens on the other side of Rome; they do not compare at all in grandeur with those of the Villa d'Este in Tivoli near Rome where the great fountains and grand cypress frame the view of the city and the country around.

The Vatican gardens' claim to beauty is the view of the dome of St. Peter's. There is no place in all the gardens where its majestic curves, designed by Michelangelo, are not framed in trees, reflected in the waters of a still pool—where the cupola does not seem to stand guard over the lovely lawns and brilliant flowers.

The fifty acres of cool green splashed with bright color stretch from the railway station on the south wall of the city all along the old Leonine wall at the "back" of the Vatican to the south where the public entrance to the Museum is located.

The gardens run right up to the extensive governor's palace; they completely surround the Ethiopian College which, as the only school inside the walls, trains future black bishops for Africa. Put down quietly in the midst of the gardens is the small Vatican broadcasting station with steel-lace towers rising above the ilex trees. The garden hides the Academy of Science, a pontifical institution that dates back to the time of Galileo. Originally the Academy was the summer casino of Pius IV. Built in 1558 for this Pope who sometimes liked to get away from his palace, it is now used only when Academy members travel to Rome to meet with the Holy Father.

The gardens are actually two gardens—the old and the new. The old gardens begun so long ago that they are lost in history are reached by the Viale della Zitella, the Street of the Spinster. Formally laid out, they are a series of vistas, broken only by the fountains that frame in silver mist the graceful dome of the basilica. The paths are irregular, lead often to boxwood inglenooks where an ancient marble or terra-cotta statue stands in a shady corner.

The governor's palace, center of civil administration for the 108-acre state

A fountain, crystal-cool on a July day

A formal Italian green garden—behind the scenes in the Holy City

The line between old and new gardens begins at a medieval watch-tower in the Leonine wall—once the watchtower of the Vatican observatory.

The new gardens are full of flowers. They have fewer trees, which makes them seem sunnier and more intensely colorful. Less formally laid out than the old gardens, they contain stretches of open green lawn and rose gardens as well as the gardens laid out in the classic Italian patterns. On

Padre Ludovico da Aquila, rector of the Ethiopian College, with a student

In the shadow of the dome, the *negretti* play a fast game of volley ball

Photograph originally taken for Look Magazine

rolling ground, their brightness enlivens the views from St. Peter's basilica, the palaces and museums. Camellias and gardenias bloom through the long warm season; lilies float in the mossy pools, flamboyant cannas are ranged against green laurel hedge. The new gardens are kept fresh and flowering by modern irrigation, one central tap controlling the crystal spray of thirty-two acres of hidden lawn fountains.

For the greater part of the day the gardens belong to all the citizens of the Holy City and are theirs to enjoy. But from three o'clock until shortly after five in the afternoon, they are ringed with guards and inaccessible. No one may enter the gardens while the Holy Father is having his afternoon stroll unless he has business at the Radio Station. There is no traffic during this period except the *negretti* of the Ethiopian College who come in from classes outside at this time, the gardeners who go unobtrusively about their work, or—occasionally—a child who wanders in by a path not properly policed.

There is one story told about a grimy urchin who found himself near the Holy Father, so near that his dirty hands and his unwashed face drew the Pope's eyes and attention.

"However did you manage to get so very dirty, my son?" asked the Holy Father, smiling.

Without a quiver and possibly without realizing to whom he spoke, the little boy answered, "Padre, if you'd been playing as hard as I have—and in that white dress—I guess you'd get dirty too!"

In the refectory at lunch—future bishops of Africa and their teachers

Citizens of the Holy City

"**Y**OU MIGHT ALMOST SAY the state of the Vatican is a state of mind," an official once said. "At least, it is like nothing else I know in all the world."

In contrast to the three to five million pilgrims the Holy City will be host to during the Holy Year, there are just under a thousand bona fide citizens in the state. Housing is so cramped between the old walls that many of these citizens live outside in Rome proper and arrive for each day's work shortly after the St. Anna Gate opens in the early morning.

Although the miniature country came into being twenty years ago, in all that time not more than a dozen of its citizens have been born on its soil. Fewer than that have been buried in the crypt of St. Anna's Church that is particularly set aside for them. As a matter of fact, the entire cemetery system of the Vatican is amazing. There are five altogether. Three of these including St. Anna's are church crypts. Only popes and cardinals may choose to be buried in the first crypt of the basilica near the supposed location of the tomb of St. Peter. No one may be laid to rest in the sub-sub crypts of early Christian and pre-Christian eras recently discovered in the lower excavation of St. Peter's Church. Swiss Guards have their own special plot behind St. Peregrino's Church but often elect to be returned to their home country after death. The Teutonic cemetery near the Gate of the Bells has

Giuseppe Cottefoglie; By Appointment—shoemaker to popes and cardinals

fallen into disuse; originally intended as a final resting place for German pilgrims who died in Rome, it has been moss-grown and untouched now for many years.

Although there is a first-aid clinic run by the Brothers of Charity who also operate the modern, first-class pharmacy, needed medical attention is usually sought outside by the citizens. They must also go to Rome to shop, to eat, except in the case of the guards' and workers' canteens, to see a movie. The little children troop out St. Anna Gate before eight-thirty each morning of the long ten-month school year to Roman schools in the neighborhood. There is but one of the many schools and colleges of the Vatican on the grounds. The tall young *negretti* of the Ethiopian College live in their own building with the Capuchin friars who are their teachers and professors in the curriculum of the Coptic church. And their school is on the grounds only because a pope in history once professed to like "seeing a bit of black mixed in with all the white."

Citizens must also go into Rome to take a train or a bus. There is no need for transportation within a country that can be covered wall to wall on foot in fifteen minutes of easy walking. But there is no passenger service out to Italy and the world from the bon-bon marble railway station.

The Vatican is not in business. There is no commerce. And no manufacturing at all. One small shop in the vicinity of the Museum sells replicas in miniature of famous Vatican statues. But business fell off so during the war that owner Luigi Mercatali is doing all the work himself these days. He expects to take on an assistant again, but only when he must get a stock ready for the Holy Year rush of pilgrims and priests who want to carry away with them some reminder or memento of the visit. In the Mosaic Studio where commercial orders are taken at any time the artists are free to work on other than church panels, prices do not include a profit to the Holy City. They are figured precisely at cost plus a percentage of upkeep of the studio.

There is almost no business enterprise among the citizens; there is no crime. There are no customs and no taxes. Vatican male citizens do no military duty. The five groups in service to the Holy Father—Swiss, Noble and Palatine Guards, Pontifical Gendarmes and Chamberlains of Cape and Sword—are all imports.

Men outnumber women citizens of the Holy City about nine to one. The women are usually the wives of the fortunate citizens who have been able to get one of the apartments in the "village," but there are a few others as laundresses, housekeepers, cooks to high-ranking officials. The sisters of St. Vincent de Paul who run the hospice and cook the great vats of spaghetti, macaroni or beans with sauce served each noonday to the workers, the six German sisters who are the private servants to Pius XII, and the nuns of the San Franciscan order who are employed in the workrooms and studios for tapestry and fabric repairs, all retain the nationality of their birth—as do the 100 Swiss Guards and 750 Italians in the country.

Citizenship in the Vatican, with its privileges, is obtained by birth or acquisition; the latter is renewable every six months by application to the

The dalle Torre babies, escorted by mother, nurse and pup, go down to the Holy City railyards to see the trains come in

Notice on a Vatican street: "Out of respect for the Lord's House and in accord with Christian precepts, ladies who live in or visit Vatican City are requested to wear stockings and dress modestly"

offices of the governor, the Marquis Camillo Serafini. As the Pope's deputy for administration of the civil affairs of the Vatican, Serafini's responsibilities are centered in the area of the "village" near St. Anna Gate and Church.

The governor, whom Pius XI appointed in 1929 as soon as there was a reason for having a governor, was once employed in the Vatican Library. He, with a staff of administrative deputies, is responsible for facilities, upkeep of grounds, the one thousand people who call the Holy City home. Housing is a problem he faces, and sometimes not too happily. Vatican apartments are free and therefore much sought after. For some years they were let more or less as bonuses to faithful workers. Accusations that this distribution was unfair and constituted an actual increase in take-home pay were frequent and a more equable system of distribution was instituted.

Marquis Serafini is in charge of the issuing of Vatican passports and the bureau of auto licenses. There are about 250 cars kept in the Vatican— owned by the Holy Father, his staff, cardinals and other dignitaries. However, almost three thousand licenses were issued yearly to personnel who

Mail delivery simplified. A Vatican housewife lowers a basket on a string

**One of the dozen "green-thumbed"
Vatican gardeners who tends the 50
acres of flowers and lawn**

**Luigi Mercatali puts the delicate
finishing touches on tiny plaster copies
of a Greek head from the Vatican Museum**

were engaged in the work of the North American College, the seminaries,
religious orders, Propagation of the Faith, and the English College—some
of which are located outside the Holy City or enjoy extraterritorial rights.
The Communists made so much of this "wide" distribution prior to the 1948
spring elections in Italy that the governor has become very strict concerning
the rules for obtaining an "SCV" for an auto, bicycle or motorbike.

Italian police never arrest a driver with a Vatican City license plate.
They may take his home address if he lives outside the Holy City, call on
him at another time and fine him *out* of his car, but the fine is likely to be
light and in the nature of a warning.

Just so, the Italian police who are on duty in St. Peter's Square are
carefully briefed as to their behavior and the necessity for careful action on

Monsignor Montini's housekeeper administers a playful reprimand to His Excellency's favorite house cat

Fabiani Amideo, for 27 years a custodian in the Vatican Library, waits at his table for another bookworm with questions

this one piece of Vatican territory where they do duty. All relations between Italy and the Vatican are exceedingly polite; difficulties in small overlapping authorities are handled with such courtesy as to make any quarrel impossible. The necessary transit visas for imports to cross Italy from the entry point—for instance, by air to Rome—are dispatched without delay. Italian police take instructions for handling huge crowds on festive days when they gather in the Piazza from the Papal Gendarmes who police the Holy City.

The Holy City, like any other geographical unit, is made up of all kinds of people—young, old, poor and well to do. Naturally, most of the citizens are Italian; but the few "foreigners" are accepted and liked. The atmosphere is always happy; everyone knows everyone else and shares with

Photograph originally taken for Look Magaz

Luigi Felici, the Pope's personal photographer, chats with one of the Pope's gaily costumed Swiss Guards

A priest and a Vatican mechanic tinker with an auto engine. Flag and license plates are marked Knights of Malta

his neighbors the preference for being where he is and doing what he is doing more than anything else on earth.

It is difficult for an American Catholic or an English or a French Catholic to imagine complaining, worrying, being unhappy because he was not certain of being given a chance to run an elevator, polish marble and bronze, scrub floors, guard relics or swing dangerously from a sixty-foot rope on a cupola inspection job. But the sons of the San Pietrini—the almost five hundred workmen who keep up the Church of St. Peter—are jealous of their fathers' jobs and anxiously hope to grow up and inherit them.

The menial jobs are many and are proudly handed down for generations of one family. *Bussolanti* who carry the Holy Father's chair hope to

Cleaning day—carpets from the Sistine Chapel are vacuumed and swept

110

have a son or a nephew who may serve someday in the same capacity. Some of the bright-eyed little Italians growing up in the Holy City, using the papal gardens as parks, sharing the only ball ground and gymnasium within the walls with the intelligent and merry African students, fill their out-of-school time running errands around the place. They hope to learn the ropes and perhaps become priests themselves.

If the temper of the Vatican workers is good, so is the pay. The cardinals' $5000 a year does not compare with what men of their talents earn in the outside profane world and they have high expenses (a complete wardrobe is very costly for a man with such a salary).

Wine for the Swiss Guards' canteen is checked over the border

Guards entertain family and friends in their muraled canteen

But below that level—and out of the church hierarchy—salaries in the Vatican average between 25 and 40 per cent higher than in Rome outside the walls. The atmosphere is not slow, but neither is it rushed. The atmosphere is one of modern facilities curiously mixed with Renaissance splendor and great pomp. On state occasions the great arched courtyards are colorful with Swiss Guards and thousands of people mill about as the papal prelates in purple gently herd them in the proper direction. On every day of the week, something is going on.

The guards and custodians in the libraries meet great scholars who come to do research; handymen in the galleries watch English, French, German, Dutch, Spanish, Brazilian tourists on their art tours, take home stories every night. Felice, the official photographer, photographs visitors of position or of importance to the Holy Father for the papal archives and for newspaper releases also. Every guard and chamberlain knows him well. Garagemen salute cardinals; chauffeurs on duty frequently speak several languages and are Vatican guides and friends to the bishops who must pay a visit once each five years back to Rome.

The conclave and visitors' housekeeping staff, in charge of all the great lot of thrones, beds, bureaus, linen, china, silver and furnishings needed to ready one wing of the palace and house the Sacred College of Cardinals should they be convoked, are local historians of importance. The carpenters, art "doctors," and conservation specialists of the Vatican know their opposite numbers from far and wide; they frequently teach classes, as do the archivists and librarians, to learned pupils from other countries.

The Vatican has a definite social life. Not on a high level because Pius XII lives a simpler and more austere life than is usual for even a pope. And not on the once-customary diplomatic level. The last of the great dinner parties for which the Vatican was once known was held twenty years ago in the palace on the occasion of the signing of the Lateran treaty creating the state; not since then has the gold plate been used or such a list of delicacies been served.

But children have birthday parties; there are family get-togethers after a christening. A resident cardinal may and does invite friends to his table. The *maestro di casa*, Commandatore Pio Manxio, likes to show off his charm-

Early Monday morning—the wash is hung out behind the Bernini columns

**A Brother of Charity fills a prescription in the Vatican
pharmacy, patronized by the Pope, the court and citizens**

ing little apartment with its porch atop the Bernini colonnade; the Swiss
Guards' canteen is never deserted of young soldiers and friends. Monsignor
Montini, Pro-Secretary of State, has very little time to himself, but his house
and Baron Bartolomeo Nogara's might be called the Vatican penthouses.
Small they are—but from their tiny roof gardens they have incomparable
views of the cupola of St. Peter's and the palaces which are shared with
guests.

The busiest place in the "village"—the hub of day-to-day social life—
is the little side street where the main post office and the Annona, the Vatican
provision store, are located.

The Annona is never empty. From seven in the morning when the first

116

housekeepers appear to buy still warm bread for breakfast until it is closed in the evening, there are people dashing in and out. Chamberlains and *bussolanti* in court dress, chauffeurs, guides, nuns, monsignori, guards, San Pietrini, cooks to cardinals, barefoot friars come to buy the ¼ litre of red or white wine allowed per day, the rationed 300 grams of fresh white bread baked in the next-door bakery, or the daily package of American cigarettes which are available at half price.

This modern provision store is decorated in gleaming chromium and glass and divided into four shops. One sells fresh fish, wine, fruits, including bananas, dates and oranges, greenstuffs trucked in from the gardens of Castelgondolfo, the papal farm of the Holy Father outside Rome. This farm equipped with the best of modern agricultural machinery—tractors, threshers, churns—kept the Vatican citizens well provided for during the war. Butter, eggs, cheese, and chickens that outsiders could not get were available to customers of the Annona.

A quart of good spaghetti—2¢. Sisters of St. Vincent de Paul feed 600 workers lunch each day in the modern Vatican canteen

Photograph originally taken for Look Magazine

**Red or white? Holy City citizens buy their daily wine
in one of the shops in the large Annona provision center**

One of the Annona shops sells fresh milk; another displays the best of Italian cheeses and olive oil, Argentine corned beef, sausages, pale-pink veal and beef, luscious hams. The so-called grocery division is where staples of jams, spaghetti in twenty sizes, macaroni, noodles and the bread, rolls and bread sticks are sold. The grocery also has shelves of excellent aperitifs and

Supermarket Vatican style—meats and cheeses at reasonable prices

brandies marked medicinal at less than fifty per cent of prices asked in Rome stores.

Down the way from the provision store is the post office. It opens about as early as does the Annona and receives its heaviest mail for distribution at seven-thirty and eleven-thirty. In a very modern building, the public room

The line forms at the right of the busy registered mail window
in the central bureau of the Vatican post-office system

**Sorting incoming mail at the post office. The *anticamera* box
is for the letters addressed to His Holiness, Pius XII**

of which looks like a bank, the post office is one of few Holy City facilities on a paying basis. Aside from the ton of mail that comes in and the one-half ton that goes out during each twenty-four-hour period, the post office handles hordes of collectors and collectors' requests for papal stamps in series. There are almost 190 different Vatican stamps; of these, the four last series are easily had—twenty-five stamps, four of which are on postal cards. The average earnings in a year may easily come to 20,000,000 lira.

Everyone may stop in at the post office to buy; the right to purchase in the Annona is rigorously limited to Vatican citizens and their dependents. The first is both a convenience to the citizens of the state and a money-making proposition; the second is a special privilege, a facility the Holy Father shares with his faithful servants and the subjects of his minute state.

Vatican Trustees

THE ROMAN CATHOLIC CHURCH has increased its world population nearly 35 per cent since 1914. In the United States alone there are now 26,800,000 Catholics—almost 700,000 more than there were at the end of 1948.

More important even than the growth in numbers is the vastly increased importance of the Church in 1950. Whether Eugenio Pacelli is Pope because of the emergence of the Catholic Church as a factor in international policies and its need for a man of his caliber—or whether this new importance is directly traceable to him no one will decide.

But, as cause or effect, Pope Pius XII is currently playing a large part in increasing the Vatican's political prestige abroad. His primary consideration is the salvation of souls; his first responsibility the formation of good and faithful Catholics. Like other pontiffs before him, the Holy Father finds his efforts in this direction seriously hampered by anti-religious political systems and armies on the move. He has had to become a fighting pope and a shepherd who shows undaunted courage.

As head of the Church, Pius XII has absolute jurisdiction over everything pertaining to church affairs—spiritual, financial, or political. He runs the world's smallest, and in some ways most powerful, state as a one-man authority. Although known as *Pastor Angelicus* (the Angelic Pastor), he has

His Eminence, Nicola Cardinal Canali—chairman of the Board of Cardinals. Behind him a portrait of Pius XI, the building Pope

123

Count dalle Torre, editor in chief of the official Vatican religious/political daily, *L'Osservatore Romano*, works at his desk on an editorial

His Excellency, the Most Reverend Monsignor Ludovico Kaas—Economo (Executive Manager) of St. Peter's Church—in his garden

proven himself a forceful, clear-thinking, hard-headed chief of state.

At present the Vatican has no Cardinal Secretary of State. The Pope has had only two young Pro-Secretaries of State on his staff since the death of his friend and one-time schoolmate Luigi Cardinal Maglione.

The Holy Father seems to have no member of any religious community to serve as his chief collaborator or to act as his principal in missionary fields in matters of law. Pope Pius XII knows the world he traveled extensively. He has caught the temper of his time and has, in many instances since his early years as nuncio in Berlin, been ahead of the game in political foresight. He speaks Latin, Italian, Hebrew, French, German, English, Spanish and Portuguese. And he speaks to twenty times as many people as any pope in the history of the oldest household servants.

His Eminence, Giovanni Cardinal Mercati—prefect
of the Vatican libraries and archives—
with the books he loves so much

Baron Bartolomeo Nogara—director general
of the Vatican museums—photographed
in his office above the Pinacoteca

The Holy Father is his own best information chief. He is a law unto himself and no one questions the ultimate rightness of the decisions and moves he must make each day.

There are about the Pope on Vatican Hill a few trusted deputies whose advice he constantly seeks, albeit without any commitment to use it. Some of these men are young, unknown outside the walls. Some are very old. They are priests and cardinals and lay members in the service of the Church. There are good business heads and tried diplomats in each group. Some are suave men of the outside world; others are scholarly, seemingly vague. All are faithful servants of the Holy Father.

Six weeks after his coronation in 1939, Pius XII set up a special Pontifical Commission, composed of three cardinals, to act as liaison between him and the details of civil administration of the Vatican. This Commission, originally intended as a kind of balance wheel for internecine duties and the sometimes resulting tensions, has gradually grown more and more important. It is headed by His Eminence, Nicola Cardinal Canali, who was for a long time ceremonial and protocol expert in the Vatican. An energetic, sharp businessman, the cardinal is adept at the art of saying "no." His position gives him frequent opportunities to practice.

The Pontifical Commission, which works closely with the governor of the state of Vatican City, His Excellency, Marquis Camillo Serafini, has been joined by a lay member and has absorbed new responsibilities outside of the Holy City itself.

His Excellency, Count Enrico Galeazzi, is the Special Delegate to the Commission as well as Director General of the Administrative and Economic Services of the Holy See. Count Galeazzi is also a successor to Bramante and Michelangelo—the Architect of the Sacred Apostolic Palaces.

Count Galeazzi's position is one of working for Cardinal Canali. His importance lies in his long and close association as a confidential advisor and friend to the Holy Father. While his name is seldom before the public, he probably knows more American Catholics than anyone in Italy. When the great Knights of Columbus playgrounds were built near the Vatican, Galeazzi—then in the lean and struggling years of his career as a builder— was discovered by Edward L. Hearn and asked to construct the grounds and operate them. In his position as a commissioner for the Knights, Count Galeazzi managed property, their offices, and received all important members.

He was promoted to the board of consulting architects for St. Peter's Church, given medals and decorations; he was made a Knight of Malta, the highest honor for a layman. He was consulted by many well-to-do foreigners who bought or leased estates in Rome. In 1936 the Count came to the United States as private chamberlain to Cardinal Secretary of State Pacelli, visited Mount Vernon, called on the Roosevelts at Hyde Park. He became part of the liaison between the Vatican and the United States.

Count Galeazzi's influence is wide and his talents are varied. He is entrusted with financial undertakings and many confidential affairs. Buying, selling, banking matters pass over his desk. It is supposed that such investments as the Vatican holdings in the *Société Anonyme* of Monte Carlo and Vatican interests in the Italian Catholic Action movie productions are his business.

The Catholic Church is sensitive to criticism that it possesses a great share of this world's goods and strives to acquire more. As a matter of actual fact, the Vatican has been lacking funds once in recent history. On the death of Benedict XV in 1914, there was not sufficient money in the treasury to finance the conclave and pay the expenses of the cardinals called to elect a new pope. The Cardinal Secretary of State borrowed the money from a bank.

Questions concerning the finances of the Holy See are met with the cold answer, "The Holy Father does not publish a budget." And it is true that there are not a half-dozen men in the world who know how much the Vatican has or where it goes.

There are five main sources of income. One is Peter's Pence—the voluntary contributions of the faithful all over the world for the maintenance of the Holy City. A second source is the rich spring of private contributions and the legacies frequently left by devout Catholics to the Church. A third is derived from the Lateran Financial Convention signed in 1929 when the Vatican became a state. In this agreement, the Holy City received $40,000,000 in cash and $52,000,000 in 5 per cent Italian bonds to compensate for the papal territories taken away in 1870 at the time of the unification of Italy. This fund is handled by a special commission including Count Galeazzi and banker Bernardino Nogara, whose brother directs the Vatican museums.

The fourth source of monies needed to run the world-wide church and often, at this particular time, to keep priests and nuns alive in the Communistic countries where their properties have been confiscated, are the investments made with the capital listed as the third source.

The fifth way the balance sheet of the Vatican is safely more black than red is from collection of the ordinary fees from the Mosaic Studio, the post office, the Museum.

Any careful examination of the financial status of the Vatican on the surface reveals a studied attempt at simplicity in living and office quarters. The great wealth that is obvious—books, manuscripts, museums crowded with art treasures, the basilica treasury of jewels and crowns and relics—is

His Eminence, Pietro Cardinal Fumasoni Biondi—head of *Propaganda Fide*

Count Enrico Galeazzi, Vatican architect and business genius

not real. That is, it would be difficult to realize money on those treasures without further depressing the financial position of the Church.

The responsibility for the riches of the Vatican have been carefully assigned. His Excellency, Monsignor Ludovico Kaas, Economo of the Basilica St. Peter and Director of the Mosaic Studios is a clever and tireless priest whose work on the excavations about St. Peter's tomb in the crypts of the basilica have already earned him a place in Vatican history. Monsignor Kaas is a German, a good friend of the Holy Father whom he has known since the Pope was a new nuncio to Berlin—fencing with a recalcitrant Kaiser over a religious concordat.

In conversation, His Excellency shows a dry and consistently wise humor. He is forthright and some of his quips are barbed. During the past decade, new duties have been added to that of caring for the great home church of St. Peter. Co-workers say his advice is usually good, always measured. Frequently among his special jobs is the reception of important people; he takes them over the cathedral, shows them the dome or the crypt work of which he is so proud. And all the while he makes the simple tour, he is speaking quietly, persuasively, in Italian, German, English or French, skillfully weaving his stories of history and church personalities. He gives St. Peter's Church some of what it seemingly gives him. For those of his guests appreciative of the treasures of the basilica he guards, nothing is too much trouble.

On one occasion a Hollywood producer named Samuel Bronston toured the basilica with Monsignor Kaas and returned then to the office of the Economo where he asked for permission to film the church and its grandeur in color. His Excellency asked Bronston, who was the producer of *Walk in the Sun*, the name of his company. Bronston replied, "I haven't any. I'm just an independent."

"Very well," answered Kaas. "Although I have hundreds of requests for the same privilege here in my files, I think I'll let you be the one."

"Why me?" queried Bronston.

The old man smiled. "You are a Jew. It's about time one of the race got what he wanted. They've been having much too much trouble."

Baron Bartolomeo Nogara is the mild, soft-voiced scholar who runs the vast Vatican museums. He takes his job seriously and, while his forte is Etruscan and early Roman art, he has backed the first timid attempts now being made to introduce some of the newer "modern" art forms into the Vatican. He has staffed his bureaus intelligently, obtained the best from all over the world in art personnel for repairs on the famous Raphael frescos and for the Vatican's never-ending search for new techniques in art repair and art protection.

His Eminence, Giovanni Cardinal Mercati, is at once the successor to Achille Ratti, who became Pope Pius XI directly from the Vatican libraries, and one of the most distinguished and colorful figures in the Vatican. Many call him the world's greatest "bookworm." He is a bibliophile of no small dimensions and his job, most successfully executed, is to keep the prestige of the Vatican book and manuscript treasures high among scholars, to insure the continuity of various Vatican codices as undisputed authority.

Cardinal Mercati is friendly, amiable—not half as formal as his dignified portraits would indicate. He handles *the* Vatican codex—the Old Testament in Greek from the fourth century—as reverently as it deserves. But his explanation of what it means to the religious and book world is made piquant with the kind of funny anecdote that children like. He keeps his vast erudition for the writing and the searching he constantly makes in order to build his libraries to greater fame.

Count Giuseppe dalle Torre, the editor of *L'Osservatore Romano,* like others in important positions in the Holy City, is thoroughly professional about his work. A brilliant newsman, he manages to turn out an official daily paper that is as informative and objective in world reportage of news events as the *Christian Science Monitor.* Of necessity there are elements in *L'Osservatore* of the court circular—special and private audiences with the Pope are always listed on the front page of the four-page afternoon edition. But dalle Torre, a papal count, manages to inject life into the editorials and keep religious and official opinions out of the news. It has been said that Pius XII, whose own speeches and writings now total ten great volumes, is dalle Torre's co-editor on the paper.

Of the twenty-one various divisions of the Roman *Curia*—the departments of the hierarchy for administration of the Roman Catholic Church's affairs—two are perhaps quite well known. Almost everyone has heard of the Roman *Rota* which is the court of appeals dealing chiefly with marriage-annulment cases. The *Index* which is a part of the Holy Office is known as a department which censors books that Catholics may own, read or sell.

The importance of these two in no wise equals the importance of the Congregation of the Propagation of the Faith or the Office of the Secretariat of State.

Propaganda Fide is the heart of the missionary effort of the Church. Headed by His Eminence, Pietro Cardinal Fumasoni-Biondi, this office has been dubbed the O.S.S. of the Church. News of conditions—political, social, religious—filters to this cardinal's desk every hour and makes his bureau the greatest information center in the Vatican. His Eminence was Apostolic Delegate to India and later to Japan; he was also for almost ten years the Delegate to Washington, D. C. And he knows from constant and close communication with the nuns, missionary fathers, bishops, teachers, in Asia, Alaska, South America, Australia, Finland, Denmark, Sweden, Norway and Africa, the underground currents that he must report to the Holy Father. His intelligence merged with that from the Sacred Consistorial Congregation, which maintains the same close relations with all countries where the Church has evolved from a missionary state to run on its own (the United States, France, Germany and countries behind the Iron Curtain) is the ammunition needed by a successful Secretariat of State.

Extending to more than sixty countries, the Vatican Secretariat of State personnel occupy positions that are public as well as religious. Nuncios are sent from the Holy See to those countries with whom there are official Vatican relations. Delegates are sent to those countries where relations are good but not official, such as the United States. Vicars are sent to missionary countries. Since the end of World War II, the situation of the Catholic Church has been such that only a *Capo-Missione,* a kind of observer, has been sent to Germany and two Americans, Monsignor Hurley in Yugoslavia and Monsignor O'Hara in Romania, are assigned to the Russian-dominated area.

The single aim of the Department of State simplifies its setup. Religion through friendly governmental co-operation or tolerance is its purpose. At the head of the department—directly and frequently responsible to the

His Excellency, the Most Reverend Monsignor Giovanni Montini— Pro-secretary of State and secretary-particular to the Holy Father

Holy Father—are Their Excellencies, Monsignor Giovanni Battista Montini and Monsignor Domenico Tardini.

Monsignor Montini is slim, hollow-eyed and occasionally forgetful. He is in charge of internal Vatican affairs and finance. Ordained a priest in 1920, he began his work low on the ladder of the department in 1924. He wrote the scholarly *Universal Conscience* during his long tenure in the busy offices of the Secretariat and today, in addition to his heavy departmental duties, is first private and extraordinary secretary to the Holy Father himself.

Duties of a full-fledged Secretary of State are shared with Monsignor Tardini who concerns himself with world-wide ecclesiastical and external affairs of the Vatican. Intellectual, logical, Tardini taught Theology at the Pontifical Academy before he became a member and then Secretary of the Congregation for Extraordinary Ecclesiastical Affairs, dealing with foreign governments in the establishment of dioceses and the working out of treaties and concordats. During Fascism in Italy he held the religious and protective post of an assistant in the great Catholic Youth Organization. He complements the great priest that Montini is.

His Excellency, the Most Reverend Monsignor Domenico Tardini—
Pro-secretary of State in charge of world-wide ecclesiastical affairs

Ring Around the Pope

OF THE TITLES borne by Pius XII, the last—and possibly least in his consideration because it is temporal—is the title of Sovereign. The Holy Father sends and receives envoys. He negotiates treaties and many times offers his services as arbiter of international disputes. Although the Vatican holds itself aloof and neutral from wars, it actively exercises its right to use moral and spiritual force. His Holiness coins money, has stamps engraved, issues passports. The international postal convention recognizes his nation and he observes copyright and patent laws.

And Pius XII has an army. Small as the Vatican is, a great part of its population is soldiers. All in all, there are five military groups in service to the Pope. Three of them are more honorary and ornamental than actual; the Noble Guards are appointed from Roman and Italian first families to serve in the antechambers as guards of the Holy Father's person. The Palatine Guard created in 1850 is made up of Roman shopkeepers, merchants and decent bourgeoisie. The Palatine is called out to parade on special occasions and it has a first-class band which plays concerts for visiting dignitaries. The Privy Chamberlains of Cape and Sword are from many countries; it is their privilege on visiting Rome to don Spanish costume with white ruff and cape for honorary short-time duty in the Pope's apartments.

The other two military organizations of the Vatican—the Swiss Guards and the Papal Gendarmes—are the Pope's crack troops. The latter are Ital-

Changing of the guard—inside the Bronze Door, a new detail takes over

ians, all taller than five feet nine, and are, in gala uniform, exact copies of Napoleon's famous grenadiers. Outside of the Hall of the Gendarmes in the Pope's palace, they are the police of the Holy City. Under the command of Colonel Francesco Bernardo, they are responsible for public order, traffic, protection of the gardens during the Pope's afternoon visit there, the palaces, churches and buildings which crowd so busily together inside the walls. On special assignments members of the gendarmerie do duty as plainclothes guards. They have their own barracks, complete with recreation room and billiard tables, in the Vatican, and they are issued ammunition as are the Swiss Guards.

The Swiss troops are widely publicized as the Pope's personal body-guard, sworn to defend his life with their own.

Back in 1505 when the Swiss were cannily playing political games with France, games that could have resulted in serious consequences to Pope Julius II, that Pontiff bestowed the honor of providing his personal troops on the Swiss-German cantons of Switzerland. Their present commander-in-chief, Baron de Pfyffer d'Altishofen, is the twenty-seventh officer and the tenth commander of that name in the 445 years of the illustrious history of the guards. The Baron has been commander since 1934.

Candidates for the bright outfit of red, yellow and blue (Medici colors introduced by a Medici pope) must be between nineteen and twenty-five years of age. They must stand five feet, eight inches or more in height, present both civil and church references of character and piety, submit to an extensive medical examination and pass the sharp-eyed examination of Baron de Pfyffer when they are called to Rome.

As first-year men they may be dismissed without reason. They are supplied a room in the barracks behind the Bernini colonnade and their uniforms —the three-color formal dress, a sixteenth-century blue costume, with knee breeches and cape for guard duty, a strange three-quarter length smock to wear when the work at hand might dirty their best, and the world's most uncomfortable gala armor. This last, reserved for very special occasions, consists of a highly polished steel cuirass with a ruff, plumed armor helmet and either a long halberd or an enormous two-handed sword.

Swiss Guards in the predominantly Italian Holy City are a small community all by themselves. They have their own miniature church dating back a thousand years where the sermons are delivered in German; their own flag with the arms of the present pontiff and those of their founder, Julius II, in the corners. In their canteen, they eat Swiss-German food and drink Italian wines. Their small cemetery, one of two above ground among the Holy City's five burial places, contains sacred earth brought from Calvary in the seventeenth century.

After three years of service, guardsmen are given a three-month furlough. Until then their families and friends may visit them in the Vatican,

In the Belvedere Court a sergeant gives gun drill to Swiss Guards

**Papal Gendarmes in gala Napoleonic dress salute a distinguished
visitor coming out from an audience with the Holy Father**

dine with them in their canteen or meet them in outside Rome for the evening.
But the guards' evenings are surprisingly short; there is a ten-o'clock curfew
in high summer and nine-thirty in spring and autumn. Nine o'clock sees the
gate locked in winter.

Corporals must serve eight to ten years; being a sergeant is the reward
of twelve years in the service. The officers may marry, but the privilege has
been withdrawn from the ordinary soldier because the Swiss-Italian sons resulting from those marriages always wanted to grow up to be guards like
their fathers. This difficulty could not be easily resolved—as guards must be
Swiss citizens at the time of their swearing in.

The Swiss Guards at full strength number 100 to 120 men. Twenty ac-

**In duty dress, a detachment of Papal Gendarmes with carbines
cross the Belvedere Court on their way to police the gardens**

company the Holy Father to Castelgondolfo on the shores of Lake Alban whenever he goes there in the summer. They are trained in the use of rifles, are expert at hand-to-hand combat. During the war they acquired a machine gun and were organizing a motor corps. Although they are a very small unit, no one ever laughs at their history of fidelity to the Pope.

During the sack of Rome on May 6, 1527, the city was stormed by Charles of Bourbon's German and Spanish mercenaries. In an attempt to capture the Pope, they attacked the unprotected Vatican where they were met by the Swiss Guards. Overwhelmingly outnumbered, the Swiss battled long and courageously with the foreign troops in an effort to keep them engaged. Nearly 150 were killed in the Square of St. Peter, on the steps of the basilica and near the main altar where the Spanish and Germans followed them. Forty-

A priest and officers of the Palatine Guard relax in conversation after a papal celebration where they paraded in full dress

Brigadiere Evangeliste, an officer of the Papal Gendarmes, at ease on the basilica roof during one of his plainclothes assignments

two in a ring around Pope Clement VII escorted him down the walled *passetto* to safety in Sant' Angelo, the fortified castle on the Tiber nearby. Their commander, with his wife, was tortured and killed in his apartments.

May 6, the anniversary of the decimation of the guards, is the annual day set aside in the Vatican for a colorful service of commemoration and for the swearing in of new guards to protect the Holy Father.

With only three interruptions in all the centuries since the troop was

Signor Fagiani Giuseppe, dean of *sediari* (chair-carriers) with one of the papal servants (left) dressed in rose-red damask

A distinguished-looking *cameriere secreto privato* (the Pope's private secretaries) talks with a diplomat to the Holy See

first formed, the guards have stood, day and night, outside the popes' doors. They are the first Vatican citizens a pilgrim sees high on the battlements of the Holy City, the first sight of Vatican color at the Gate of the Bells, the Bronze Door, or the St. Anna Gate.

The closer ring around the Pope—his housekeeping staff, his valet, his private secretaries and the *decano* (chief butler), are the last people outsiders ever see. These few know the Holy Father as the "I'll have it my way" master of his household. Their chief function is to keep him well dressed, properly fed, and, if possible, relaxed for the little time he has to himself. All this they are supposed to do without once stepping beyond the bounds of good

144

servants, without seeming to have their minds on anything more than the mechanical tasks in front of them. Chosen for tact, age, experience and the poise necessary to work at such close quarters with a reigning pontiff, they are an unusual group. Protocol and their positions naturally forbid confidences to outsiders. But their pride is so great that they cannot help occasionally relaxing to the point of telling a little. And what they tell reveals a deep concern for the welfare of the man they serve.

His kitchen nuns when buying at the Annona are more particular than any housewife about the quality of the ham or cheese that is being cut for them. They cannot accept less than the very best of provisions.

His valet, Stephanori, has a complex about drafts. He follows the Holy Father with extra wraps and coverings on almost every occasion. In the spring when the great official rooms of the Apostolic Palace seem overwarm and crowded with too many pilgrims in audience, Stephanori waits unobtrusively at the doorway—where, when the Holy Father passes through, he can neatly toss a tiny ermine cape over his shoulders.

His private secretaries, like the guards on duty in the Square below his apartments, despair over the hours the Holy Father keeps, worry to each other when the light burns past two o'clock. They have been known to sit dozing for long late hours in the anterooms when the Holy Father wrestled with the composition of an important speech. Even when not asked to stay on duty, they feel they may relieve him of some work if they are at hand when called.

They, like many others, want to be directed, wish to be of use, hope— and sometimes express aloud that hope—that the answer to some of the pressing problems of being alive today can be explored and indicated by the selfless man they serve and surround.

The Holy Father as Others See Him

I<small>N ALL THE WORLD</small> of those who feel closely and intimately bound to Rome, there are none who are tied more closely or depend more on the children-to-father relationship than the Italians.

The first time a visitor to the Vatican hears a crowd of nearly 100,000 in St. Peter's Square chant *"viva il papa, viva il papa,"* he will be thrilled. But on a great state occasion, such as an anniversary mass in the Sistine Chapel, when the same cry goes up from young students and priests, Roman children, housewives, members of the press who line the corridors of the palace to see the Holy Father pass, that pilgrim if he comes from a non-Latin country may wonder at the propriety of the demonstration.

There is something in the cry akin to the enthusiasm shown at a football rally—or the cheering section of an international match. But this is a surface resemblance.

Beneath what appears shocking and uninhibited, there is a little lesson in semantics. The Pope is the Pope in English; the word is a title. In Italian or French, he is father, papa. And there lies the reason his person is venerated and he himself so much loved. Those who feel close to the Holy Father think of him as a human who has taken unto himself, through years of prayer and work and study, the attributes of a saint in this world. And they feel he has done it for them.

Pius XII is many things to many men. He is usually what the pilgrim,

His Holiness, Pius XII, being carried in his *sedia gestatoria* through the
Sala Ducale on the anniversary of his coronation as Pope

147

the supplicant, the diplomat, the student, the priest or nun or child expect to find.

On some occasions his courage and dignity, his poise, or his lively humor have been more than the visitors expected. In the autumn of 1918, when Archbishop Eugenio Pacelli was nuncio at Munich, his house was invaded one evening by a gang of armed marauders.

The nuncio was working on the top floor of the official residence on the Brennerstrasse when he became aware from shouts and crashes of furniture below stairs that one of the robber groups terrorizing the city was paying him a call. Quietly and very quickly he left his desk for his bedchamber. Here he put on his purple silk robes before starting down the stairs.

With his staff lined up behind him, Eugenio Pacelli descended to meet the strangers, praying as he went. At the turn of the stairs, the little group looked into the barrels of five rifles the hoodlums had leveled at them. The nuncio made the sign of the cross and continued down. Suddenly, as he stopped, the rifles were lowered. In precise German he then asked, "What do you want?"

"Money, jewels—all your food," replied the leader, with a slight nervousness.

"Why are you armed? We have no guns and no one here will harm you."

The men shuffled their feet and looked quickly from Monsignor Pacelli to their leader. "We may have to harm you, kill *you*," he said.

"Why kill me? I am not your enemy."

"You have what we need. Where is all the stuff? The food? The money?"

The purple-robed priest became a little more sure of himself, and bolder. "We have only a little sugar and butter and flour here—just sufficient for ourselves. You may not have it. You must leave. This is the legation of the Holy Father. You are on Vatican property; in this house you are *in* the Vatican itself. I order you to leave."

The men seemed to grow smaller after this gentle, firm speech from the tall man on the steps. They turned and halfway to the door yelled, "Where's your auto?"

"In the garage," returned Pacelli.

At the head of a papal procession, cardinals carry the
cross and tiaras—symbols of the Pope's authority and position

Hand raised in the traditional gesture, the Pope blesses pilgrims

"Well, we will take that," snapped the leader, dashing from the house.
During World War II, the Germans arrived in Rome. They sent a task
force complete with machine guns, mortars, antitank cruisers, into St. Peter's
Square. A bluff, gruff major took command and, although he was on Vatican territory, no formal protest was made by the calm Pope who was con-
vinced that his greatest protection lay in no protection at all.

From his windows Pius XII could see German guards at the Vatican

Members of a visiting French choir take pictures of the Holy Father during Mass

frontiers examining the papers of all who went in or out. He could hear the commands shouted at the changing of the battalion. He refused to receive General Kesselring in audience, but he did see the German ambassador.

"Holy Father," said Baron von Weizsacker, "I have been instructed by the Führer to assure you that the German Army is here only to protect Your Holiness."

The atmosphere was tense. Quietly and sternly, the Holy Father spoke. "I have placed my protection under the symbols of my faith. My crucifix will be more protection to me than all the tanks in your army. We would be better pleased if you would take them all away."

Later the ambassador returned to the Holy City to inform the Pope that the Nazi soldiers must stay. He suggested that there were lawless elements among the Italians of the city and protection against them was necessary.

"We have ourselves walked among the people," observed the Pope. "Everywhere we were respected."

The Holy Father referred to several instances which had earned him the reputation in Rome of "antiaircraft Pacelli." On July 19, 1943, a secretary was hurriedly summoned to the private office of His Holiness.

"Quickly. Order an automobile right away. No retinue. There has been a bombing in the San Lorenzo quarter near the station. Get all the cash money together that we have. We will withdraw it personally from the cashier." The cashier had only two million lira; another two million were taken from the safe of the *Fabbrica* of St. Peter's Church. Before the all clear had sounded, the Holy Father was among the weeping, shocked survivors of the raid. His face whiter than his gown, he knelt among the wounded, trying to give them comfort while his chamberlain distributed money for food and hospitalization. Several hours later when the crowd that collected about him finally parted and withdrew to let him go back to his car, his secretary saw his hands and his white robes were purpled and stained with blood.

The day following the liberation of Rome, several representatives of the Allied press personnel who had arrived with the armies called on the papal *maestro di camera* and asked if an audience with the Holy Father could be arranged. When asked how many of the press wanted to meet the Pope, the two reporters making the plan estimated about thirty-five.

On the morning the audience was granted, the number was closer to a hundred. Allied reporters had told Allied photographers. And they all turned up in battle dress.

It is said that when His Holiness, escorted by his chamberlains, walked into the room set aside for his visitors and saw their costumes (which for the women present were rough G.I. boots, trousers tucked into the tops, khaki blouses and trench caps), he rocked back slightly on his heels and closed his eyes for a moment.

Quickly covering his surprise, he smiled a greeting and turned to

Spectators wait for the Holy Father to pass by

The Pope appears at his study window
to bless the crowds in St. Peter's Square

correspondent Eleanor Packard who was kneeling at his left. Just then, from the far side of the room, a short rumpled photographer shouted, "Hold it, Pope!" and jumped upon the papal throne while the Holy Father, smiling cheerily, "held" for his picture.

The press policy of the Vatican has improved consistently under the direction of democratic Pius XII. Radio reporters and moviemen once were shunned; photographers were taxed on the pictures they took; correspondents excluded from the colorful ceremonies.

Today, the Holy Father allows great freedom and privilege to those of the press he truly believes are the representatives of a world-wide public. Seating space and tickets of admission are fairly distributed to the press rep-

A young guard greets a lovely visitor as she comes from private audience with the Pope

Before a public audience, *bussolanti* check visitors' names against the official list

resentatives for gala occasions. Radio pickups and photographers, complete with flash bulbs, have been permitted in the basilica. His Holiness broadcasts over the Vatican Radio with increasing frequency; he has personally figured in a news telecast for the United States prepared in the Holy City. During the autumn of 1949, the first color movie of the basilica of St. Peter and inside the Vatican was allowed to be filmed. It will be released during the Holy Year 1949-50 for the millions of people who cannot make the pilgrimage to Rome.

A few years ago in a speech he delivered consecutively in seven languages, Eugenio Pacelli told the International Congress of Catholic Newsmen and Journalists, "You are the fighters." As Pius XII, his consideration for news reporters has won the Vatican firm friends.

Not until they saw for themselves, in great ceremony and in homely

The Holy Father is especially interested in his very young visitors

small receptions, the easy informality and close attention bestowed on every visitor to the Pope did they understand or appreciate the democratic bearing of the man. Rich and poor, Christian, Jew or Hindu, important or humble— they are received with the same grace.

A country priest came to the Pope one morning in 1942. "Holy Father," he begged, "give me a special blessing for my soldiers. I have four hundred."

"For yours that are four hundred and for mine that number millions," said His Holiness, "the blessings and protection of our Father in Heaven."

Nuns from hospitals bring their crucifixes to audience that they may have the blessing; some pilgrims carry so many rosaries and souvenirs to be blessed by the Pope that they have difficulty genuflecting. Not infrequently a family in trouble or in flight from the country that displaced them will arrive at an audience in tears, with painful secrets they feel they must reveal. The Holy Father usually takes them to a corner where their confidences will not be overheard and listens as long as it takes to tell the story, making notes, nodding his head as he gives all his attention.

Children are immediately drawn to the Pope. And he to them. In large springtime audiences held in the Belvedere Courtyard for Italian schoolchildren, the Holy Father is as gay and smiling as he is ever seen. The children are jubilant, the chaperoning nuns and priests relaxed when all goes according to plan. Sometimes even the rather dour papal chamberlains remember to look happy.

Those received in the antechambers with smaller groups have seen amazing and amusing things happen. Once the Holy Father stood lost in the story of a mother who held in her arms a little girl wearing leg braces;

Rosaries and medals are brought for the Pope's blessing

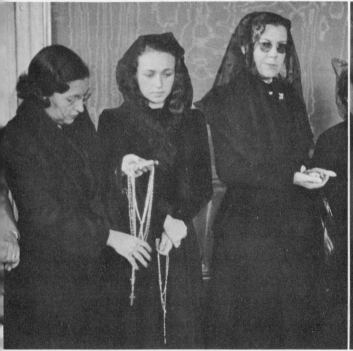

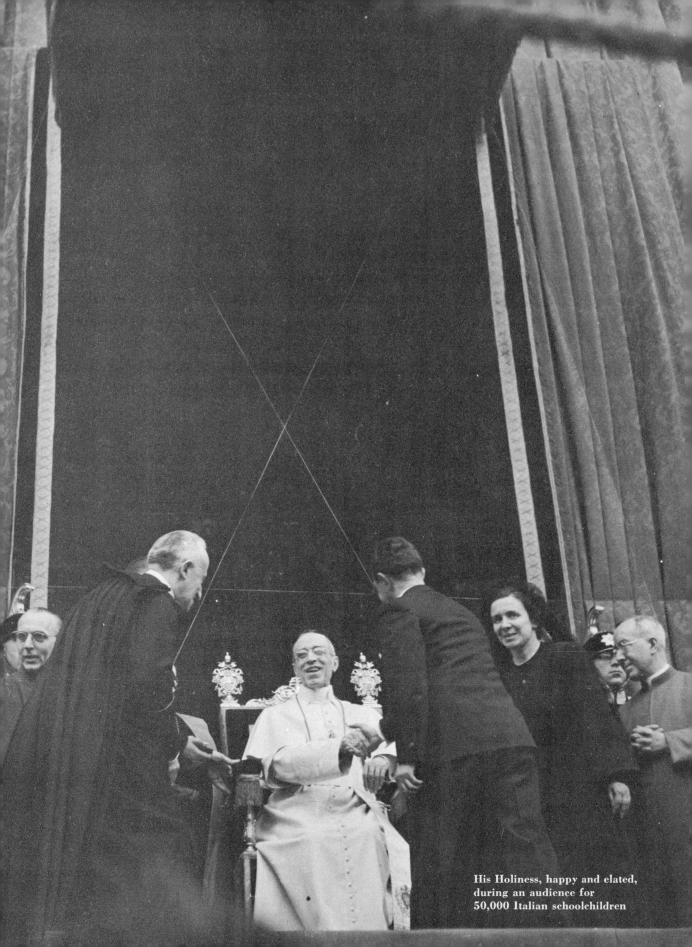

His Holiness, happy and elated,
during an audience for
50,000 Italian schoolchildren

for twenty-five minutes the *maestro di camera* fidgeted at the time passing while the Pope stroked the child's silvery blond hair and patted her cheek.

Another time, the Holy Father was ending an audience with a blessing on all those gathered in the Sala Clementina. Just as he turned to the door where his valet waited with a cape for his shoulders, a strange cry went up from an old woman in the back of the room. Attendants started to hustle her from the group, thinking to solve the disturbance out of the Pope's hearing. The little white-haired Italian woman would have none of it, struggled away from them and dashed for the Holy Father.

She was sobbing when he reached her. Falling on her knees, she held out to him the beautiful fisherman's ring he wears on his right hand. It had slipped from his long narrow fingers as she kissed it and she had held it shaking with fear of disturbing the pilgrims until the audience was completely finished.

Ordinarily a visitor to the Pope for the first time remembers nothing of what he saw before he saw the Holy Father himself. Coming up from the deep genuflection that is etiquette on presentation, the visitor is greeted in the language which is checked as his next to his name and whispered to Pius XII at the moment of greeting. It is not at all strange to see solid citizens, poised businessmen, adult women of education and experience, tremble when they actually are in the presence of the Pope. Kindly his smile and blessing may be, but his dignity, his bearing, are overwhelmingly impressive. His vivid black eyes are searching.

They relax a little after he goes on to others in the line, are interested spectators as the Pontiff passes from one language to another—bends to children, questions the priests who have come from a distance, helps a very frail old lady up from her curtsey.

On the way out from the reception rooms, visitors pass by Noble Guards on duty in the Hall of the Tapestries, by a picket of Palatine Guards in another great antechamber, by the Hall of Gendarmes where the tall soldiers stand rigidly at attention. Chamberlains bustle about busily, *bussolanti* and papal lackeys are on duty in the little dark cloakroom where gloves, coats, handbags are carefully stored. And finally the pilgrim has caught his breath and reaches familiar ground again with the sight of a full platoon of the

Swiss Guards who are drawn up in the Clementine Hall.

Diplomats and personages rate a standing salute and presentation of arms from the colorful Swiss. The Holy Father is saluted from bended knee whenever he passes with his papal court.

On the Sunday morning, February 20, 1949, when Pius XII stood on the balcony over the imposing front entrance of the basilica of St. Peter and told the hundreds of thousands listening in the square below him of the plight of his faithful Cardinal Mindszenty in Hungary, he was white and upset as he began to talk. He grew stronger and more defiantly concise as he delivered his message but his face stayed pale until, with tears in his eyes, he gave his blessing to "the city and the world" and retired to his private chapel to pray.

At Easter time or in March when the Holy Father celebrates his birthday and the anniversary of his coronation, the faithful throng into St. Peter's Church to see him in the full trappings and panoply of his position. Borne high above the heads of the crowd on his *sedia gestatoria*, he wears the triple crown and gold-embossed cape. His chair is carried by the *bussolanti* in red damask; they are flanked by bearers of the great white ostrich fans. Members of the purple-gowned *anticamera* precede him; cardinals and members of the court follow. The great center aisle to the high altar of St. Peter's is lined with his honor guards.

From the moment the Holy Father kneels at his prie-dieu behind the altar until the Mass is finished, all eyes are fastened on him. None of his movements lack grace or significance. No part of the ceremony of the Mass is performed perfunctorily. Because of his deep and moving spiritual power, he holds his audience and bestows on the onlookers some of what the sacrament and prayer mean to him.

Pius pp. XII

His Private World

THE PRIVATE WORLD of the Holy Father is very small. As the infallible spiritual leader of three hundred and fifty million Roman Catholics, he belongs to them. His private life is limited. To have any at all, he must get up very early or stay up very late. He does both—the time he has before he leaves his chamber in the morning and greets his valet or the hours after midnight when he is apt to send his private secretaries off to bed are all that he keeps for himself.

Before he was Pius XII, Eugenio Pacelli was the widely traveled Cardinal Secretary of State. He was gregarious, enthusiastic, curious. He saw the world and loved every minute he spent with people, singly or en masse. He called on kaisers, kings, presidents; toured, as no one of the hierarchy of the Vatican before him had ever done, the United States of America, South America, England and continental Europe.

All this was changed on March 2, 1939. For twenty-four hours the sixty-two cardinals of the Sacred College had been on their appointed thrones in the Sistine Chapel for the purpose of electing the Vicar of Jesus Christ to succeed Achille Ratti, Pope Pius XI. There were two ballots taken and the vote was scattered. In both cases—as custom demands—the ballot papers were burned with wet straw in the small cook-stove installed for the purpose. The black smoke produced by this conflagration told the thousands

A country vista in the Holy Father's favorite corner of the gardens

restlessly waiting in St. Peter's Square that no decision had been reached.

The third vote was unanimous with one exception. Eugenio Pacelli voted against himself. But when the Cardinal Bishops asked him to accept, he murmured a slow "yes" and bowed his head.

And then the cardinals lowered the canopies over their thrones until the only one in the room still up was over the head of Pius XII, Bishop of Rome, Vicar of Jesus Christ, Successor of the Prince of Apostles, Supreme Pontiff of the Universal Church, Patriarch of the Occident, Primate of Italy, Archbishop and Metropolitan of the Province of Rome, Sovereign of the

166

State of Vatican City, now Gloriously Reigning.

The third and final ballots were burned—this time without straw. The quick puffs of white smoke from fast-flaming paper signified to the crowds outside that a new Pope had been chosen. As the muffled roar from the Square reached the Sistine Chapel, the Holy Father disappeared into the adjacent robing room. There he found new white soutanes in three sizes waiting. The middle size fit, and he was helped to change from his cardinal's robes into the severe, caped white wool cassock.

When he had changed, Pius XII appeared on the central balcony of the basilica of St. Peter and gave his blessing *Urbi et Orbi* (to the city and the world) over a storm of cheers—*"Viva il papa . . . viva il papa."*

From that moment until his death, he will be charged with the vast responsibilities of his office. He will be surrounded with the tradition and ritualistic trappings of the Vatican, governed in most of his actions by protocol centuries old.

He can do no entertaining as a private individual. He eats all of his meals alone, but he never leaves his private apartment in the palace without an escort. He may not travel. He stays within the walls of his miniature 108-acre city-state except for brief retreats or an occasional summer removal to the papal villa at Castelgondolfo near Rome.

Although audiences are held to very small numbers and life is more informal in the country, he will never have a vacation from his heavy duties.

The Holy Father has no peers. Even those few remaining friends with whom he studied for the priesthood and those of his intimate family are but obedient servants.

His life is lonely. His opportunities to be with other people as a person do not exist. Although he loves children so much that he taught catechism at the Nuova Chiesa all his few free hours during a difficult apprenticeship in the Secretariat of State, he has no time now to be with his own great-nieces or great-nephews.

Pius XII has such concern for the spiritual welfare of people that he gives unstintingly of his waking hours to audiences and leaves his desk work and study until nighttime. Only a great strength that is obviously not physical strength allows him to work as hard as he does, the hours he does, in a whole-souled attempt to preserve peace by diplomacy and the good offices of his Church.

His Holiness is extraordinarily intelligent. He has a brilliant mind and a background of experience in world affairs which no pontiff in history rivals. His perception and fine political sense have made him humbly aware that decisions he makes profoundly affect the destiny of the entire world— his own people, people of other religions, people of no faith at all.

In his selfless attempt to achieve lasting good results in the name of the Roman Catholic Church, the Holy Father makes a constant and stubborn effort to simplify his own life. He delegates to others many duties which are pleasant and interesting—but time-consuming. He has cut his private pleasures to the minimum, made austerity a principle of his existence.

Although he can discuss music with Yehudi Menuhin—and has surprised Mr. Menuhin with his knowledge—he no longer touches his violin. While his taste is trained and he is appreciative of paintings and art forms, he permits himself no interest at all in the Vatican museums. He consults with Baron Bartolomeo Nogara, prefect of the galleries, only on the budget needed to run them and preserve their treasures. He will not read a book for his own personal enjoyment.

Unlike Pius XI who was a building pope in the remarkable way of Sixtus and Julius before him, Pius XII spends none of his energies on architectural improvements of his temporal realm. The one building to his credit is the canteen for the day laborers of the Holy City; that he ordered built because he frankly thought it of advantage to labor relations.

Pope Pius XI is supposed to have spent many days on the roof of St. Peter's basilica in 1929, during the final stages of treaty arrangements which were to end his exile and give him real property again. In those days when conversations between Cardinal Secretary of State Gasparri, Avocato Francesco Pacelli, Mussolini and/or his deputies were concerned with the boundaries of the tiny nation, Pius XI made plans with his architects. They could not walk over the ground not yet theirs so they surveyed it from the air 400 feet up on St. Peter's porches. The round, merry little Pope from the north knew just how he wanted the little kingdom of the Vatican to look when it was completed.

His successor, Pius XII, is scarcely aware of how it does look. He may have the deep feeling for green and growing things all Italians have, but he has neglected to appropriate monies for the world-famous Vatican orchid collection. It has gone to seed. The greenhouses Pius XI often checked personally are dilapidated, are little more than potting sheds today. To the despair of some of the proud Italian gardeners, this Pope has made no changes nor suggested any improvements to the acres laid out centuries ago and greatly added to by the last Pope.

During the Holy Father's afternoon walk in the garden, he is preoccupied. Frequently he begins his excursion at a fast pace, thin shoulders stooped, head bowed. After a little he may wander from the canopied walk to look at his favorite pool beneath the fir and cypress, but he seems to gaze beyond and through the beauty that surrounds him.

Private secretaries who sometimes accompany him believe the Holy

**Back of the Radio Station, near the old Vatican walls—
the protected path where the Pope walks on rainy or cold days**

Father is relieved when the airing is finished—that he has done what the doctor ordered only to return to his work a little rested.

Commandatore Angelo Stoppa, the chauffeur who drives the Holy Father from the palace half a mile to the policed gardens each afternoon, also drives him when he goes to Castelgondolfo. Stoppa, with only a few others, has seen the Pope relaxed and happy to escape from the city.

Once the smart black 1948 Cadillac is on the road outside Rome, it is not unusual for His Holiness to pick up the speaking tube and order speed. "Faster, faster," he says. As he sits in the single, fawn-upholstered chair in the center of the back seat, the Holy Father smiles, blesses those who kneel in recognition of the tiny gold-and-white silk papal flags or the

Commandatore Angelo Stoppa, chauffeur to popes since 1922

Parked in the garage door, the Pope's 1948 Cadillac gets a high polish

RAEDIS·PONTIFICVM·SERVANDIS

Garage interior: here an antiquated Mercedes Benz,
a Citroen and the gilt and plush horse-drawn
carriages are neatly filed away.
Above: Urban's state coach which was
permanently retired from use in 1870

SCV-1 license plate, and enjoys his outing completely. He fiddles with the dials of the radio which is concealed in two cabinets flanking his comfortable chair. If lively, rhythmic modern music results, he is inclined to let it play on and gently nod his head in perfect time with the beat.

The Cadillac which is Stoppa's great joy runs up mileage very slowly; at the end of a year's use less than 3500 miles had been clocked on it and it looked as shiny as the day it arrived.

Only slightly less new are the other vehicles occupying space in the white-tiled garage off the Belvedere Court. Stoppa arrived with the first machine, in 1922. He is the first and only official Vatican chauffeur to popes and in this position is the autocrat of the garage. His daily duties are light and most of his time is spent overseeing the two "juniors" in the service whose task it is to keep the "wheels in the service of the Pontiff" looking their best. The first little Fiat which made its debut in the Holy City with Stoppa at the wheel is gone. But the rich, red velours-lined Citroen, the low-slung Mercedes Benz, and the Graham-Paige with the pink velvet throne are lined up according to their age. (The Graham-Paige is still used when a visiting cardinal needs a car; it bears a No. 1 license plate.)

Behind them are the fourteen gilt and velvet state coaches, silver-mounted saddles, and, in the free space at the back of the garage, bundles and boxes of food and clothing shipped from the Catholics of America for distribution by the Holy Father to the needy. On an order from a secretary or from one of the nuns who care for the household of Pius XII, Stoppa will take crates or boxes to the rail station and reroute them in answer to a plea that has reached the Pope's desk.

Three hundred days of the year Commandatore Stoppa's routine is the same. He waits to drive the Holy Father to the gardens in the afternoon.

Three hundred days of the year—more or less—the schedule of Pius XII is the same. The only variety is provided by the number he receives in great public audiences or by the position or personality of those he sees privately. As his public and state life is very much arranged by the *maestro di camera,* so his private life is kept running smoothly by the *maestro di casa,* Commandatore Pio Manzia. As Master of the Household, the Commandatore has a most unusual housekeeping job. His huge staff of grooms,

Commandatore Pio Manzia, *left, Maestro di Casa*—master of the household—
in conversation with Colonel Bernardo of the Papal Gendarmes

lackeys, chair-carriers, butlers, the Holy Father's personal valet, Giovanni Stephanori, and the six German nuns who have attended the Pope since he was nuncio in Berlin during World War I take orders from him. The Commandatore is also go-between for the tailor, the shoemaker, who fits the Holy Father's arch supports, Stoppa at the garage, the Pope's private physician, the *camerieri* of importance from other countries who, on visits to Rome, are privileged to share in the honorary duties of the Cape and Sword group.

"Housekeeping for His Holiness isn't as complicated as you might think," says Manzia when questioned. "The Holy Father is not demanding."

At six o'clock in the morning, His Holiness wakes in his austerely simple bedroom. It is unusual for his valet to find him still sleeping when he knocks at six-fifteen. Although the plain brass bed has, by order, a thin and hard mattress, Pius XII sometimes sleeps on the board floor.

Because the Pope is rather nearsighted, his first gesture when he wakes is to grope on the bedside table for his spectacles. After bathing and quickly dressing in the robes laid out the night before by valet Stephanori, the Holy Father goes to one of the windows to open it and look out on St. Peter's Church and the Square. Cold weather and bad, he can usually be counted on to appear a few minutes before seven o'clock. Although protocol provides an hour and a half for a Pope's toilet, Pius XII has managed to cut it to forty-five minutes.

On one occasion shortly after the Allied armies arrived in Rome, the Holy Father observed a reporter and a photographer with a telephoto lens waiting for him to look out his window. Usually, he is more than obliging to the press, but on this occasion he shut himself in his room, and dispatched a guard with the message that "before breakfast is too early—even for the press and the Pope."

The bath is as luxurious as the bedroom is spartan. It was refurbished along with the rest of the apartments during the first few months after Pius XII's election as Pontiff while he continued to live in his old Secretary of State rooms on a lower floor of the palace. The large room is full of American and British knobs, buttons, special shower equipment—shiny chrome gadgets that contrast sharply with the exterior of the old palace. His Holiness is not attended while bathing, shaving or dressing although his valet waits in the next room for the sound of the bell which would call him if the Pope needed assistance or were taken ill. The Holy Father uses an electric razor—one from a gift collection of Italian, English and American models.

In 1939 and 1940, a deal of physical culture apparatus was installed in the bath. Since his heart attack in 1946, the Holy Father has not used the dumbbells or exercisers on advice of his doctors, all of whom protest any strenuous activity. They have, on occasion, protested against eighteen-hour working days as well. With almost no effect. The Holy Father pays very little attention. Although he is past 73 and weighs less than 150 pounds—too little for a man 5 feet 11 inches tall—he stubbornly continues to fast and abstain, to get up and stay up as he wishes.

A few minutes after seven in the morning, the Holy Father is in his small workroom next to his chamber. Here he reads the lesson for the day and then begins to read and write memos. At seven-thirty sharp he goes into his small private chapel to celebrate Mass with the priest who is his confessor.

From the chapel he goes down the corridor to the dining room. It contains a dark wooden table, six chairs (five of which are usually empty) and a serving bureau. Pius XII eats in solitude. Pius XI always invited members of his intimate family and household to supper around Christmastime, but the present Pope has gone no further than to ask several who work with him to join him at supper for conversation. They do not break bread with him.

Food for the Pope's table is cooked by two of the six German nuns who have managed the kitchen, laundry, and housekeeping for the Holy Father since his days as nuncio in Berlin. He sends them to Castelgondolfo in the summer—and refuses to eat unless they have prepared the meal. The valet de chambre brings the simple meals from the pantry to the dining room and then disappears.

For breakfast, the Holy Father has rolls or *croissants* with coffee that is half hot milk, Italian style. For lunch, he has some kind of a light entree, a grilled chop or small steak, fruit and wine. At dinner, he likes a green salad and fish or new vegetables cooked with a little oil and some *pasta* with a bit of cheese. The *pasta* can be noodles, spaghetti, macaroni or any one of a dozen in the line the Annona carries, but it must be cooked at the last minute before serving and it must be "*al dente*"—something to bite into.

At eight-thirty, the Holy Father takes his private elevator down to the second floor where the secretaries and chamberlains are already waiting. The heavy mail sent over from the Vatican post office at seven-thirty has been opened and sorted. Urgent letters and messages are divided among the secretaries with instructions to report back later in the day. By nine o'clock, His Holiness is ready for the half-dozen newspapers he reads—including the Communist Rome daily. Shortly after nine-thirty he receives his own news reports from the editors of the official Vatican newspaper *L'Osservatore Romano*. He may go over special editorials with editor-in-chief Count dalle Torre or with writer Professor Lolli.

The *maestro di camera* is eventually admitted to advise the Pope of the audiences that have been arranged for the morning. The present substitute *maestro di camera*, with his staff, are in complete charge of the Holy Father's morning time from this point on.

As quickly after ten o'clock as the office staff have their assignments in hand, the Holy Father is free to begin his audiences. First on the list come the private, diplomatic and most important visitors. Semi-private and then larger public audiences follow. By mid-morning, Pius XII can be counted on to have wrecked the time scheduling and be on his way to being late again for lunch.

Pius XII is a listener. He will listen for an hour if his visitor can report on another country, has an intelligent idea or news of any of his far-scattered flock.

On those occasional days when the audiences are finished before one-thirty lunch, the Holy Father rests upstairs for fifteen minutes before eating. When he is very late, he sits at table quietly reading while the sisters boil another batch of spaghetti and broil a new chop. After lunch he rests another few minutes or visits the chapel.

From two-thirty until four o'clock, the Pope receives reports from missions, heads of congregations. He may see the Cardinal Prefect of the Propagation of the Faith, the head of the administration of the basilica, or

President of the Vatican Council, Cardinal Canoli. Monsignor Tardini and Monsignor Montini, Pro-secretaries of State, have their appointments, give reports, receive advice. Throughout the whole palace, there is a feeling of alertness during the early afternoon. Anyone in the Secretariat of State, the governor's palace, the libraries or museums may be summoned to see the Holy Father.

Precisely from four to five, Pius XII is in the gardens.

From five until an eight-o'clock dinner, the Pope will see his doctor, his nephew, a personal friend. He is accessible to any of his secretaries or deputies with questions and problems and during this period of the day, the gold-and-white telephone on the right side of his large desk rings frequently. When the secretary puts through such a call—and all calls are screened— it is certainly someone the Holy Father knows. His salute has always been *"Aqui, Pacelli."* (Pacelli here.)

The large private office is impressive. There are three great recessed windows that give on St. Peter's Square. They are draped in beautiful gold damask but the curtains are rarely pulled; when the light becomes too strong the slatted white inside shutters are closed. Decorated for the present Pope, the room, 60 by 40 feet, is paneled in soft blond wood. Most of that half of the room farthest from the door looks unused. There are tables and satin chairs rather well distributed on the carpet; the walls are lined with books to the level of the eye and paintings above—but its formal air is very different from the corner of the room by the door. Here, five feet to the right of anyone entering, is the desk of the Holy Father. Behind it, a high-backed white satin chair with a gold-stenciled wood frame. In the chair there is a small, sausage-shaped, gold satin kidney pillow. Ringed in a half-circle in front of the desk are six or eight smaller red satin armchairs. Visitors seated in them have a clear view across the desk to the Holy Father because he keeps his books and papers far to the right of a mounted crucifix, neatly stacked near the telephone. His typewriter and dictaphone rest on smaller tables to his right.

Against the legs of a table, on the floor behind the red chairs, there is a large oil of Jesus of the Bleeding Heart. It has obviously been placed where it is, in easy sight, on the Holy Father's direction.

Young students man the Vatican's telephone switchboard day and night

Sometimes the atmosphere of a clearing house is broken in the later afternoon and the Pope will put aside his memos, direct the telephone be cut off, and receive some caller who has been unable to come to him during the usual hours audiences are granted. Only high government officials or a foreign diplomat, occasionally Premier of Italy di Gaspari, who was a Vatican librarian for ten years during Fascism, are granted the favor of an out-of-hours visit.

After his simple evening meal, the Pope retires to his private chapel or to his apartments for an hour. About nine—or a little after—he is ready to begin his day's work. The hours that follow, that end toward morning, are given to considerations, decisions, speeches, letters—the concerns of his spiritual children all over the world.

The switchboard. Stoppered lines in upper left corner are the Pope's private wires—and are never used for incoming calls

His Larger World

Carved over the entrance of the small radio power station standing in a far corner of the Vatican gardens is an inscription. It reads "In order that the voice of the Supreme Pastor, by the ether waves, for the glory of Christ and the salvation of souls, may be heard to the ends of the world."

Designed by Marconi and supervised by him until his death in 1937, Station HVJ has been actively on the air since 1931 when it was completed, assigned international wave lengths and scheduled transmission hours. It is modern to the very last detail and it has the powerful transmitters necessary to carry the voice and commissions of the Holy Father over the earth.

Missionaries in from the field—visiting Rome from Africa, the Orient, an island remote from the home base—report with strong emotion the reception of a broadcast from the Vatican. The broadcast begins with the sounding of St. Peter's great bell, followed by the words, "Praised be Jesus Christ." Any message after that is a message straight from headquarters. It is exactly as if the Holy Father himself were telling them what to do next.

During the war the radio of the Holy City was made a general facility. Day after day, questions, to the extent of over a hundred thousand a year, as to the whereabouts of refugees, missing-in-action or prisoner-of-war personnel were sent short-wave to papal officials throughout the world. The

The steel-lace towers of the Vatican radio station built by Marconi

answers, glad or sad, were passed on to the anxious mothers and families who waited for definite word.

After the general daily broadcasts made in many languages, the most important function of the radio is the transmission of addresses by Pius XII. The radio is also used like a telegraph; data, orders and information are broadcast constantly from the offices of the Secretariat of State to the nuncios and Vatican diplomats at their posts in more than sixty countries. At agreed-upon hours, officials abroad are at their short-wave receiving sets waiting for instructions. Their problems may be dealt with generally and broadly— referring to such and such a letter of this or that date and telling them to proceed along the lines suggested. If the affair has no great political or religious significance, the orders may be direct and open.

But no matter in what terms the answers to the questions of the servants of the Church are couched, it can safely be said the answers are those of the Holy Father. Leaving little to chance, he employs the late and quiet hours when he works alone to study the wealth of material at hand, dealing with the problems of his faithful. Important decisions are left until His Holiness has found the time to think. When bishops, cardinals, legates are to be appointed, the Holy Father spends days poring over their records and the recommendations of their superiors and associates.

Although in making a public address Pius XII appears to speak extemporaneously, this is the careful effort of a practiced orator. The speeches are written or dictated with infinite care. In the final concentrated editing, the present Pontiff is able to memorize his written words and thoughts so efficiently that, although he speaks without rereading, he rarely departs one clause from his original.

When the now-famous Mindszenty address was being prepared, advisers and secretaries made themselves available at midnight. Papers, files, secretaries waited in anterooms until the Holy Father himself became conscious of the hours passing and sent them all home. He worked on alone until dawn; only Stephanori, the valet, waited with him.

Pius XII is a pope with several "firsts" for the record. He is the first pontiff to have ever visited the United States of America, three times been sent to England officially, represented the Holy See at church congresses

Radio communication center—connecting link between Rome and the world

in South America, France, and countries now in Russian-dominated south-east Europe. He is the first Cardinal Secretary of State to have been elected to the papacy in more than two hundred years. He is the first Roman pope born in the "shadow of the dome" in centuries.

He is also the first pope in modern history whose whole adult life has been lived in wars—or the backwash of world devastation from those wars.

During the first ten years as the 262nd successor to St. Peter, Pius XII has watched the homelands of nearly 15 per cent of his communicants fall to the Communist advance in southeast Europe and Asia. He has watched —and protested—the open persecution of his priests, nuns and teachers. His cardinals have been imprisoned, his cathedrals confiscated, hospitals and schools closed. Millions of his spiritual children have been denied religious freedom.

From his post of vigilance in the Holy City, Pope Pius XII has used every weapon of peace to fight what he considers a determined effort to undermine the power of the Church he serves.

From the high altar in St. Peter's basilica, over the Vatican radio, by pastoral letter and the threat of excommunication, the Holy Father has made known the lines of the Church's battle against heresy and moral corrosion.

L'Osservatore Romano, the official Vatican daily newspaper, and the Polyglot Press with which it shares modern equipment and presses, turn out a vast stream of printed material instructing Catholics and their priests on the dangers of atheism and the problems facing the Holy Roman Church.

The small office of the Vatican telephone system is staffed day and night with young student priests. At all hours in the office there is the steady, running chant of *"Vaticano. Si. Subito. Vaticano. Pronto. Si. Vaticano."* (The Vatican. Yes. Quickly. The Vatican. Right. Yes. The Vatican.) It has been estimated that there are nearly 12,000 outgoing calls each day—twice as many as are incoming. More than one hundred long-distance calls are placed through the Holy See switchboard each twenty-four hour period; many more are placed through Rome's central office. The Secretariat of State telephones are never left unattended.

Study of modern techniques of the press, radio and cinema is considered so important in high Vatican circles that a special university to teach these techniques has been founded recently in Rome. A two-year college giving a diploma in the Science of Public Opinion, the International University Pro Deo, has a wide curriculum in political science, psychology, economics, public relations. Its more than a thousand students from more than a dozen countries are taught in French, English and Italian. They enjoy modern laboratory and workshop courses in the forming of public opinion.

Quite some significance is attached to this project. His Holiness, Pope

Early afternoon edition of the Vatican daily, *L'Osservatore Romano,* comes off the press. Plant director Padre Fedeli is in the center

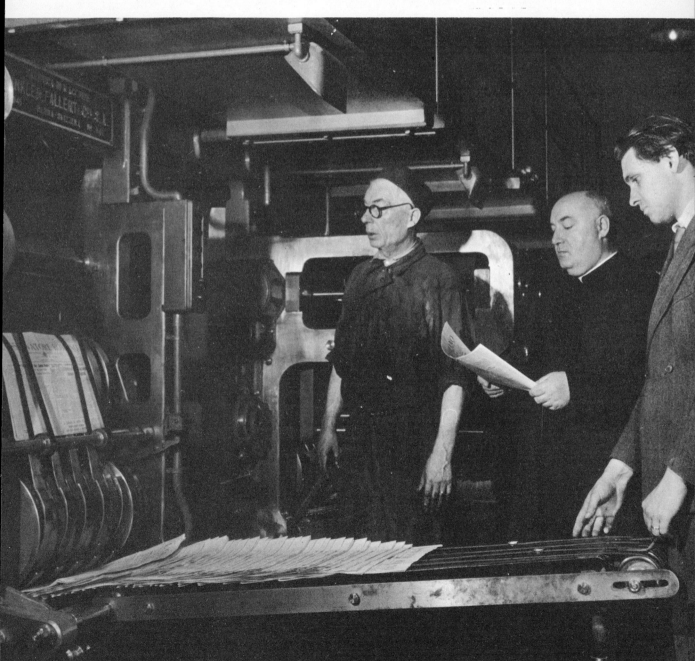

The Holy Father's "children"—one quite young, the other very old

Pius XII, pointed out at the time of the opening of the school that journalism was one of the most effective and useful means of illuminating public opinion, a means he employs with intelligence.

The balance sheet of the frail, tireless Pope at the beginning of the twenty-fifth Holy Year 1949-50 is not complete. It can serve as an indication only of what an inspired diplomat and a dedicated priest may do, must do in an attempt to deflect the current.

In spite of a somewhat general decline in religious standards in many Catholic countries and the war of principles between the Vatican and Communism, the Holy Father sees great hope in many directions. Behind the Church is a history of almost unbelievable strength and stability. Many changes have taken place in the centuries and it dominates a smaller *proportion* of the civilized world than it did in the sixteenth century, but the Church of the twentieth century is almost identical with the early Church. It has been centered on the same geographical spot for two thousand years. It teaches the same doctrine Peter taught. It holds out the same hope.

Church diplomats are realists. With a record of indestructibility and a history of such continuity behind it, there is no reason to suppose that the Holy Roman Church cannot withstand another assault.

As an elder statesman, securely grounded in the Church's modern international policies—policies he helped formulate—the Holy Father draws encouragement from the success in Catholic mission fields and in established areas such as Belgium, France and Eire. Reaffirmation of faith and piety are of great importance in countries like these three because they are countries of "saturation," i.e., there are few chances to make converts.

Successful efforts of the Vatican in establishing new relations with backsliding Mexico, Hindu India, Moslem Egypt, Lebanon and Palestine are heartening. But the deep and honest concern of the Vatican for other faiths in trouble has not blinded them to the importance of the Catholics of the United States of America. The Church finds its strength today in free-wheeling democracies where religious freedom is cherished and every man's choice respected.

The almost 27,000,000 Catholics in the United States are one of the great hopes for the battle ahead. Although in many respects they are more reactionary than the Catholics of the Catholic countries of Europe, their organizations, wealth, smoothly running press, their thousands of colleges and schools, earn them one of the greatest responsibilities of modern times.

It is acknowledged by reliable Vatican sources that the increase of the numbers of converts in this country is of great importance. But this importance is secondary to the intelligence and education and ability to think that American Catholics can apply to their faith. And think they must if theirs is the strength that is to compensate the Holy See for their recent losses in Asia, Yugoslavia, Czechoslovakia, Romania, Poland, Hungary, Latvia, Esthonia.

More than 1500 priests have disappeared in these countries. Others have been killed or fled their posts as the Communists came down into China.

It is expected that the tense situation existing in both Italy, where fewer people attend Mass than did ten years ago, and Spain, where religious bans are being eased a little, may be absolved by improvement of the levels of economic health and education.

There is no doubt in the highest Church hierarchy that the recent edict against communion and church privileges for Communists was a necessary and urgent step. Piux XII, by drawing his battle line in Italy where Communists have already lost huge numbers since the advent of the European Economic Administration, has shown both daring and prudence. Germany is a country on the line—on the border between hope for a decent revival of Catholic press and Catholic Youth Organizations and despair over Socialist prejudice against the Church.

Catholics and non-Catholics may well register the value to progressive one-world thinking and shared world-responsibility of a Church as large, as long-lived as the Church of Rome. . . . a Church that shows every sign of emerging as a dynamic factor in twentieth-century diplomacy.

If the spiritual richness of the miniature city of the state of the Vatican and the great human wisdom of Eugenio Pacelli continue to be at the disposal of all those who recognize them for what they are, the nearing hour of testing may not be so dark.

During the day, the Pope looks from his office on the Bernini fountains

At night, citizens of the Vatican see lights burning late in the Pope's private study